"*Dangerous Calling* is a dangerous book to read. It is also a book every person in ministry should read. It will cut you to the heart and bring massive conviction if you read it with humility and ask God to expose sins deeply hidden in your soul. It cuts, but it also provides biblical remedies for healing. I would love to put this book in the hand of every seminarian who walks on my campus."

Daniel L. Akin, President, Southeastern Baptist Theological Seminary

"Our wives, children, and the members we serve will have a new husband, father, and pastor by Friday if we follow Tripp's example and give a humble and honest reading of this book—one with our inner Pharisee and scribe turned off. We will see the need to save ourselves from a very dark and destructive force working against pastors: undiagnosed pastoral self-righteousness. With much wisdom and conviction, Tripp's *Dangerous Calling* preaches the gospel of grace to the men who are preaching the gospel Sunday after Sunday to everyone but themselves."

Eric C. Redmond, Assistant Professor of Bible, Moody Bible Institute; Associate Pastor, Calvary Memorial Church, Oak Park, Illinois

"Pastoral ministry is a dangerous calling, and this is a dangerous book. It will not leave you unchanged. Pastors need pastors, and, by God's grace, every page of this book will minister to your heart, your marriage, your family, and the people you serve—in ways you never thought you needed. This book digs down into the inner recesses of our hearts to reveal our greatest idols and to point to our greatest needs. It will make you joyfully uncomfortable and, by God's grace, will bring you to your knees in tears of thankfulness, only to help lift your weary head to fix your renewed gaze on Christ. This book is like a mirror that redirects our hearts' reflection from ourselves to Christ. If this book were a sermon, it would be the most weighty and refreshing sermon you've ever needed to hear. My sincere hope is that it will be translated into multiple languages, become required reading in seminaries, and be distributed to Christians everywhere who know they're called to serve God and others using the gifts with which the Holy Spirit has equipped them."

Burk Parsons, Pastor, Saint Andrew's Chapel, Sanford, Florida; editor, *Tabletalk* magazine

"Few would regard a pastor's role as a dangerous calling, but few people are as qualified and insightful as Paul Tripp to penetrate the snares and potential pitfalls associated with pastoral ministry. Fewer still would prescribe such gospel-based and local church–rooted remedies. This excellent volume should be read, re-read, and applied."

Terry Virgo, founder of Newfrontiers

DANGEROUS CALLING

Other Crossway Books by Paul David Tripp

Awe: Why It Matters for Everything We Think, Say, and Do

Come, Let Us Adore Him: A Daily Advent Devotional

New Morning Mercies: A Daily Gospel Devotional

Parenting: 14 Gospel Principles That Can Radically Change Your Family

Sex in a Broken World: How Christ Redeems What Sin Distorts

A Shelter in the Time of Storm: Meditations on God and Trouble

What Did You Expect? Redeeming the Realities of Marriage

Whiter Than Snow: Meditations on Sin and Mercy

DANGEROUS CALLING

CONFRONTING THE UNIQUE CHALLENGES OF
PASTORAL MINISTRY

PAUL DAVID TRIPP

WHEATON, ILLINOIS

Dangerous Calling: Confronting the Unique Challenges of Pastoral Ministry

Published by Crossway
1300 Crescent Street
Wheaton, Illinois 60187

Cover design: Dual Identity inc.

First printing 2012

Reprinted in Trade paperback 2015

Printed in the United States of America

Trade paperback ISBN: 978-1-4335-4137-7
PDF ISBN: 978-1-4335-3583-3
Mobipocket ISBN: 978-1-4335-3584-0
ePub ISBN: 978-1-4335-3585-7

Library of Congress Cataloging-in-Publication Data

Tripp, Paul David, 1950-
Dangerous calling : confronting the unique challenges of pastoral ministry / Paul David Tripp.
p. cm.
Includes bibliographical references and index.
ISBN 978-1-4335-3582-6 (hc)
1. Pastoral theology. I. Title.
BV4011.3. T75 2012
253—dc23 2012015795

Crossway is a publishing ministry of Good News Publishers.

LB 29 28 27 26 25 24 23 22 21 20 19
17 16 15 14 13 12 11 10 9 8 7 6 5

To all the pastors who have cared for me.
The imprint of your hands is still on me,
and I am grateful.

CONTENTS

INTRODUCTION

Books are penned for many reasons. There are *explanatory books* written to help you understand something that has left many people confused. There are *encouraging books* written to speak into the discouragement of life in a fallen world and give you motivating hope and a reason to continue. There are *instructive books* that help you know how to do something that you need to do but simply don't know how. There are *exegetical books* that take apart a portion of God's Word, helping you to understand it and to live in light of its truths. There are ways in which the book you are about to read has elements of all four of these types of books, yet that isn't meant to be its main focus.

This is a *diagnostic book*. It is written to help you take an honest look at yourself in the heart- and life-exposing mirror of the Word of God—to see things that are wrong and need correcting and to help you place yourself once again under the healing and transforming power of the gospel of Jesus Christ. Of the books that I have written, I found this one the hardest to write, not because of the writing process itself but because its pages expose the ugliness of my own heart and display how desperate my need for grace continues to be. It is not an exaggeration to say that I wept my way through writing some of the chapters. There were moments when I would go upstairs to share what I had written with Luella, the tears of conviction would come, and I would be unable to continue. But as I did my writing, it did not leave me feeling discouraged or hopeless but, rather, with a deeper hope in the gospel and a greater joy in ministry than I think I have ever known.

This book is written to confront the issue of the often unhealthy shape of pastoral culture and to put on the table the temptations that are either unique to or intensified by pastoral ministry. This is a book of warning that calls you to humble self-reflection and change. It is written to make you uncomfortable, to motivate you toward change. At points it may make you angry, but I am convinced that the content of this book is a reflection of what God has called me to do. Perhaps we have become too comfortable. Perhaps we have quit examining ourselves and the culture that surrounds those of us who have been called to ministry in the local church. I think that, more than any other book I have written, I wrote this book because I could not live with not writing it. And I have launched myself on a ministry career direction to get help for pastors who have lost their way.

I guess that means I am a pastor who is so bold as to assume that you, like me, need pastoring and, at least in the pages of this book, I will attempt to pastor you. I do that knowing that every warning I put before you I need myself, and each dose of the medicine of grace I give you I need to take as well.

It is the gospel of the grace of the Lord Jesus Christ that makes possible the honesty that is on the pages of this book. If all the sin, weaknesses, and failures that this book addresses have been fully covered by the blood of the Lord Jesus Christ, then we can break the silence, walk out into the light, and face the things that God is calling us to face. My prayer is that this book would get a conversation started that will never stop and that it will lead to changes that have been needed for way too long.

I would simply ask that as you read, you deactivate your inner lawyer and consider with an open heart. Be so bold as to ask God to reveal in you what needs to be revealed and to give you the grace to address what needs to be addressed. And as you do these things, celebrate the grace that has been lavished on you that frees you from the burden of having to pump up your righteousness to yourself and to parade it before others. Because your standing before your Lord is based on the righteousness of Another, you can stand before a holy God and admit to your darkest secrets and own your deepest failures and be unafraid, knowing that because of the work of Jesus, the one to whom you confess will not turn his back on you but will move toward you with forgiving, rescuing, transforming, empowering, and delivering grace. This is the good news not only that makes this book possible but also that you and I need to preach to ourselves and to one another day after day.

Paul David Tripp
April 10, 2012

PART 1
EXAMINING PASTORAL CULTURE

CHAPTER ONE

HEADED FOR DISASTER

I was a very angry man. The problem was that I didn't know I was an angry man. I thought that no one had a more accurate view of me than I did, and I simply didn't see myself as angry. No, I didn't think I was perfect, and, yes, I knew I needed others in my life, but I lived as though I didn't. Luella, my dear wife, was very faithful over a long period of time in bringing my anger to me. She did it with a combination of firmness and grace. She never yelled at me, she never called me names, and she never called me out in front of our children. Again and again she let me know that my anger was neither justified nor acceptable. I look back and marvel at the character she showed during those very difficult days. I found out later that Luella had already been putting together her escape plan. No, she wasn't planning to divorce me; she just knew that the cycle of anger needed to be broken so that we could be reconciled and live in the kind of relationship that God had designed marriage to be.

When Luella would approach me with yet another instance of this anger, I would always do the same thing. I would wrap my robes of righteousness around me, activate my inner lawyer, and remind her once again of what a great husband she had. I would go through my well-rehearsed and rather long list of all the things I did for her, all the ways I made her life easier. I'm a domestic guy. I don't mind doing things around the house. I love to cook. So I had a lot of things I could point to that assured me I was not the guy she was saying I was and that I hoped would convince her that she was wrong as well. But Luella wasn't convinced. She seemed more and more convinced that she was right and that change had to take place. I just wanted her to leave me alone, but she wouldn't, and frankly that made me angry.

In ways that scare me now as I look back on them, I was a man headed for disaster. I was in the middle of destroying my marriage and my ministry, and I didn't have a clue. There was a huge disconnect between my private persona and my public ministry life. The irritable and impatient man at home was a very different guy from the gracious and patient pastor our congregation saw in those public ministry and worship settings where they encountered me most. I was increasingly comfortable with things that should have haunted and convicted me. I was okay with things as they were. I felt little need for change. I just didn't see the spiritual schizophrenia that personal ministry life had become. Things would not stay the same, if for no other reason than that I was and am a son of a relentless Redeemer, who will not forsake the work of his hands until that work is complete. Little did I know that he would expose my heart in a powerful moment of rescuing grace. I was blind and progressively hardening and happily going about the work of a growing local church and Christian school.

When being confronted, I told Luella numerous times that I thought she was just a garden-variety, discontented wife. I told her that I would pray for her. That helped and comforted her! Actually, it did the opposite—it depicted two things to her. It alerted her to how blind I was, and it reminded her that she had no power whatsoever to change me. The change that was needed would take an act of grace. Luella was confronted with the fact that she would never be anything more than a tool in God's powerful hands.

But God blessed Luella with the perseverant faith that she needed to keep coming to me, often in the middle of very discouraging moments. What I am about to share next is both humbling and embarrassing. On one occasion, as Luella was confronting me with yet another instance of my anger, I got on a roll and actually said these deeply humble words: "Ninety-five percent of the women in our church would love to be married to a man like me!" How's that for humility? Luella very quickly informed me that she was in the 5 percent! How blind does one have to be to let a statement like mine roll out of one's lips? God was about to undo and rebuild the heart and life of this man, and I did not know I needed it and had no idea that it was coming.

My brother Tedd and I had been on a ministry training weekend and were on our way home. I never thought that a single trip up the Northeast Extension of the Pennsylvania Turnpike could be so momentous. Tedd suggested that we try to make what we had learned over the weekend practical to our own lives. He said, "Why don't you start?" and then proceeded to ask me a series of questions. I think I will celebrate what happened next for ten million years into eternity. As Tedd asked me questions, it was as though God was ripping down curtains and I was seeing and hearing myself with accuracy for the first time. There is no way that I can overstate the significance of the work that the Holy Spirit was doing at that moment in the car through Tedd's questions.

As God opened my eyes in that moment, I was immediately broken and grieved. What I saw through Tedd's questions was so far from the view of myself that I had carried around for so many years that it was almost impossible to believe that the man I was now looking at and hearing was actually me. But it was. I couldn't believe what I saw myself doing and heard myself saying as I recounted scenarios in answer to Tedd's questions. It was a moment of pointed and powerful divine rescue, a bigger moment than I was able to grasp in the shock and emotion of the moment. I don't know if Tedd knew at the time how big this moment was, either.

I couldn't wait to get home and talk with Luella. I knew the insight I was being given was not just the produce of God's using Tedd's questions; it was also the result of Luella's loving but determined faithfulness for all of those trying years. I am a man with a lively sense of humor, and I often enter the house humorously, but not this night. I was in the throes of life-altering, heart-reshaping conviction. I think Luella knew right away that something was up by the way I looked. I asked her if we could sit down and talk, even though it was late. As we sat down I said, "I know you have been trying for a long time to get me to look at my anger, and I have been unwilling. I have always turned it back on you, but I can honestly say for the first time that I am ready to listen to you. I want to hear what you have to say."

I'll never forget what happened next. Luella began to cry; she told me that she loved me, and then she talked for two hours. It was in those two hours that God began the process of the radical tearing down and rebuilding of my heart. The most important word of the previous sentence is *process*. I wasn't zapped by lightning; I didn't instantly become an unangry man. But now I was a man with eyes, ears, and heart open. The next few months were incredibly painful. It seemed that my anger was visible everywhere I looked. At times it seemed the pain was too great to bear. That pain was the pain of grace. God was making the anger that I had denied and protected to be like vomit in my mouth. God was working to make sure that I would never go back again. I was in the middle of spiritual surgery. You see, the pain wasn't an indication that God had withdrawn his love and grace from me. No, the opposite was true. The pain was a clear indication of God's lavishing his love and grace on me. In this trial of conviction, I was getting what I had so often prayed for—the salvation (sanctification) of my soul.

I will never forget one particular moment that took place months after that night of conviction and rescue. I was coming down the stairs into our living room, and I saw Luella sitting with her back to me. And as I looked at her, it hit me that I couldn't remember the last time I had felt that old ugly anger toward her. Now, I want to be candid here. I'm not saying that I had risen to a point in my sanctification where I found it impossible to experience a flash of impatience or irritation; but that that old, life-dominating anger was gone. Praise God! I walked up behind Luella and put my hands on her shoulders, and she put her head back and looked up at me, and I said to her, "You know, I'm not angry at you anymore." Together we laughed and cried at the same time at the beauty of what God had done.

NOT ALONE

I wish I could say that my pastoral experience is unique, but I have come to learn in my ministry travels to hundreds of churches around the world that, sadly, it is not. Sure, the details are unique, but the same disconnect between the public pastoral persona and the private man is there in many, many pastors' lives. I have heard so many stories containing so many confessions that I have carried with me grief and concern about the state of pastoral culture in our generation. It is the burden of this concern, coupled with my knowledge and experience of transforming grace, that has driven me to write this book.

There are three underlying themes that operated in my life, which I have encountered operating in the lives of many pastors to whom I have talked. These underlying themes functioned as the mechanism of spiritual blindness in my life, and they do in the lives of countless pastors around the world. Unpacking these themes is a good way to launch us on an examination of places where pastoral culture may be less than biblical and on a consideration of temptations that are either resident in or intensified by pastoral ministry.

1) I LET MINISTRY DEFINE MY IDENTITY.

It is something I have written about before, but I think it is particularly important for people in ministry to understand. I always say it this way: "No one is more influential in your life than you are, because no one talks to you more than you do." Whether you realize it or not, you are in an unending conversation with yourself, and the things you say to you about you are formative of the way that you live. You are constantly talking to yourself about your identity, your spirituality, your functionality, your emotionality, your mentality, your personality, your relationships, etc. You are constantly preaching to yourself some kind of gospel. You preach to yourself an anti-gospel of your own righteousness, power, and wisdom, or you preach to yourself the true gospel of deep spiritual need and sufficient grace. You preach to yourself an anti-gospel of aloneness and inability, or you preach to yourself the true gospel of the presence, provisions, and power of an ever-present Christ.

Smack-dab in the middle of your internal conversation is what you tell yourself about your identity. Human beings are always assigning to themselves some kind of identity. There are only two places to look. Either you will be getting your identity vertically, from who you are in Christ, or you will be shopping for it horizontally in the situations, experiences, and relationships of your daily life. This is true of everyone, but I am convinced that getting one's identity horizontally is a particular temptation for those in ministry. Part of why I was so blind to the huge disconnect between what was going on in my public ministry life and my private family life was this issue of identity.

Ministry had become my identity. No, I didn't think of myself as a child of God, in daily need of grace, in the middle of my own sanctification, still in a battle with sin, still in need of the body of Christ, and called to pastoral ministry. No, I thought of myself as a *pastor.* That's it, bottom line. The office of pastor was more than a calling and a set of God-given gifts that had been recognized by the body of Christ. "Pastor" defined me. It *was* me in a way that proved to be more dangerous than I would have thought. Permit me to explain the spiritual dynamics of all this.

In ways that my eyes didn't see and my heart was not yet ready to embrace, my Christianity had quit being a relationship. Yes, I knew God is my Father and that I am his child, but at street level things looked different. My faith had become a professional calling. It had become my job. My role as pastor was the way I understood myself. It shaped the way I related to God. It formed my relationships with the people in my life. My calling had become my identity, and I was in trouble, and I had no idea. I was set up for disaster, and if it hadn't been anger, it would have been something else.

It's no surprise to me that there are many bitter pastors out there, many who are socially uncomfortable, many who have messy or dysfunctional relationships at home, many who have tense relationships with staff members or lay leaders, and many who struggle with secret, unconfessed sin. Could it be that all of these struggles are potentiated by the fact that we have become comfortable with looking at and defining ourselves in a way that is less than biblical? So we come to relationship with God and others being less than needy. And because we are less than needy, we are less than open to the ministry of others and to the conviction of the Spirit. This sucks the life out of the private devotional aspect of our walk with God. Tender, heartfelt worship is hard for a person who thinks of himself as having arrived. No one celebrates the presence and grace of the Lord Jesus Christ more than the person who has embraced his desperate and daily need of it. But ministry had redefined me. In ways I now find embarrassing, it told me that I was not like everyone else, that I existed in a unique category. And if I was not like everyone else, then I didn't need what everyone else needs. Now, if you had sat me down and told me all this specifically, I would have told you it was all a bunch of baloney; but it was how I acted and related.

I know I am not alone. There are many pastors who have inserted themselves into a spiritual category that doesn't exist. Like me, they think they are someone they're not. So they respond in ways that they shouldn't, and they develop habits that are spiritually dangerous. They are content with a devotional life that either doesn't exist or is constantly kidnapped by preparation. They are comfortable with living outside of or above the body of Christ. They are quick to minister but not very open to being ministered to. They have long since quit seeing themselves with accuracy and so tend not to receive well the loving confrontation of others. And they tend to carry this unique-category identity home with them and are less than humble and patient with their families.

The false identity that many of us have assigned to ourselves then structures how we see and respond to others. You are most loving, patient, kind, and gracious when you are aware that there is no truth that you could give to another that you don't desperately need yourself. You are most humble and gentle when you think that the person you are ministering to is more like you than unlike you. When you have inserted yourself into another category that tends to make you think you have arrived, it is very easy to be judgmental and impatient. I heard a pastor unwittingly verbalize this well.

My brother Tedd and I were at a large Christian-life conference listening to a well-known pastor speak on family worship. He told stories of the zeal, discipline, and dedication of the great fathers of our faith to personal and family worship. He painted lengthy pictures of what their private and family devotions were like. I think all of us felt that it was all very convicting and discouraging. I felt the weight of the burden of the crowd as they listened. I was saying to myself, "Comfort us with grace, comfort us with grace," but the grace never came.

On the way back to the hotel, Tedd and I rode with the speaker and another pastor, who was our driver. Our pastor driver had clearly felt the burden himself and asked the speaker a brilliant question. He said, "If a man in your congregation came to you and said, 'Pastor, I know I'm supposed to have devotions with my family, but things are so chaotic at my house that I can barely get myself out of bed and get the child fed and off to school; I don't know how I would ever be able to pull off devotions too'—what would you say to him?" (The following response is not made up or enhanced in any way.) The speaker answered, "I say to him, 'I'm a pastor, which means I carry many more burdens for many more people than you do, and if I can pull off daily family worship, you should be able to do so as well.'" Maybe it was because he was with a group of pastors, but he actually said it! There was no identifying with the man's struggle. There was no ministry of grace. Coming from a world this man didn't understand, he laid the law on him even more heavily, as sadly I did again and again with my wife and children.

As I heard his response, I was angry, until I remembered that I had done the very same thing again and again. At home it was all too easy to mete out judgment while I was all too stingy with the giving of grace. But there was another thing operating that was even more dangerous. This unique-category identity not only defined my relationship with others but also was destroying my relationship with God.

Blind to what was going on in my heart, I was proud, unapproachable, defensive, and all too comfortable. I was a pastor; I didn't need what other people need. Now, I want to say again that at the conceptual, theological level, I would have argued that all of this was bunk. Being a pastor was my calling, not my identity. Child of the Most High God was my cross-purchased identity. Member of the body of Christ was my identity. Man in the middle of his own sanctification was my identity. Sinner and still in need of rescuing, transforming, empowering, and delivering grace was my identity. I didn't realize that I looked horizontally for what I had already been given in Christ and that it was producing a harvest of bad fruit in my heart, in my ministry, and in my relationships. I had let my ministry become something that it should never be (my identity); I looked to it to give me what it never could (my inner sense of well-being).

2) I LET BIBLICAL LITERACY AND THEOLOGICAL KNOWLEDGE DEFINE MY MATURITY.

This is not unrelated to the above, but it's enough of a different category to require its own attention. It is quite easy in ministry to give in to a subtle but significant redefinition of what spiritual maturity is and does. This definition has its roots in how we think about what sin is and what sin does. I think that many, many pastors carry into their pastoral ministries a false definition of maturity that is the result of the academic enculturation that tends to take place in seminary. Permit me to explain.

Since seminary tends to academize the faith, making it a world of ideas to be mastered (I will write about this at length later in this book), it is quite easy for students to buy into the belief that biblical maturity is about the precision of theological knowledge and the completeness of their biblical literacy. So seminary graduates, who are Bible and theology experts, tend to think of themselves as being mature. But it must be said that maturity is not merely something you do with your mind (although that is an important element of spiritual maturity). No, maturity is about how you live your life. It is possible to be theologically astute and be very immature. It is possible to be biblically literate and be in need of significant spiritual growth.

I was an honors graduate of a seminary. I won academic awards. I assumed I was mature and felt misunderstood and misjudged by anyone who failed to share my assessment. In fact, I saw those moments of confrontation as part of the persecution that anyone faces when he gives himself to gospel ministry. Now, the roots of this are a deep misunderstanding of what sin and grace are all about. You see, sin is not first an intellectual problem. (Yes, it does affect my intellect, as it does all parts of my functioning.) Sin is first a moral problem. It is about my rebellion against God and my quest to have for myself the glory that is due to him. Sin is not first about the breaking of an abstract set of rules. Sin is first and foremost about breaking relationship with God, and because I have broken this relationship, it is then easy and natural to rebel against God's rules. So it's not just my mind that needs to be renewed by sound biblical teaching, but my heart needs to be reclaimed by the powerful grace of the Lord Jesus Christ. The reclamation of my heart is both an event (justification) and a process (sanctification). Seminary, therefore, won't solve my deepest problem—sin. It can contribute to the solution, but it may also blind me to my true condition by its tendency to redefine what maturity actually looks like. Biblical maturity is never just about what you know; it's always about how grace has employed what you have come to know to transform the way you live.

Think of Adam and Eve. They didn't disobey God because they were intellectually ignorant of God's commands. No, they knowingly stepped over God's boundaries because they quested for God's position. The spiritual war of Eden was fought on the turf of the desires of the hearts of Adam and Eve. The battle was being fought at a deeper level than mere knowledge. Consider David. He didn't claim Bathsheba as his own and plot to get rid of her husband because he was ignorant of God's prohibitions against adultery and murder. No, David did what he did because at some point he didn't care what God wanted. He was going to have what his heart desired, no matter what.

Or think what it means to be wise. There is a huge difference between knowledge and wisdom. Knowledge is an accurate understanding of truth. Wisdom is understanding and living in light of how that truth applies to the situations and relationships of your daily life. Knowledge is an exercise of your brain. Wisdom is the commitment of your heart that leads to transformation of your life.

Even though I didn't know it, I had walked into pastoral ministry with an unbiblical view of biblical maturity. In ways that now scare me, I thought I had arrived. I viewed myself as being way more mature than I actually was. So when Luella would lovingly and faithfully confront me that I was just being defensive, by definition I thought she was wrong. And increasingly I was convinced that she was the one with the problem. So I didn't see myself as needy, and I was not open to correction, and I would use my biblical and theological knowledge to defend myself. I was a mess, and I had no idea.

3) I CONFUSED MINISTRY SUCCESS WITH GOD'S ENDORSEMENT OF MY LIFESTYLE.

Pastoral ministry was exciting in many ways. The church was growing numerically, and people seemed to be growing spiritually. More and more people seemed to be committing to this vibrant spiritual community, and we saw battles of the heart taking place in people's lives. We founded a Christian school, which was growing and expanding its reputation and influence. We were beginning to identify and disciple leaders. It wasn't all rosy, and there were moments that were painful and burdensome, but I started out my days with a deep sense of privilege that God had called me to do what he had called me to do. I was leading a community of faith, and God was blessing our efforts. But I held these blessings in the wrong way. Without knowing that I was doing it, I took God's faithfulness to me, to his people, to the work of his kingdom, to his plan of redemption, and to his church as an endorsement of me. It was a "I'm one of the good guys and God is behind me all the way" perspective on my ministry, but more importantly on myself. In fact, I would say to Luella (and this is embarrassing, but important to admit), "If I'm such a bad guy, why is God blessing everything I put my hands to?" God was acting as he was not because he was endorsing my manner of living but because of his zeal for his own glory and his faithfulness to his promises of grace for his people. And God has the authority and power to use whatever instruments he chooses in whatever way he chooses to use them. The success of a ministry is always more a picture of who God is than a statement about who the people are that he is using for his purpose. I had it all wrong. I took credit that I did not deserve for what I could not do; I made it about me, so I didn't see myself as a man headed for disaster and in deep need of the rescue of God's grace.

▲ ▲ ▲

I was a man in need of rescuing grace, and through Luella's faithfulness and Tedd's surgical questions, God did exactly that. What about you? How do you view yourself? What are the things you regularly say to you about you? Are there subtle signs in your life that you see yourself as being different from those to whom you minister? Do you see yourself as a minister of grace in need of the same grace? Have you become comfortable with discontinuities between the gospel that you preach and the way that you live? Are there disharmonies between your public ministry persona and the details of your private life? Do you encourage a level of community in your church that you do not give yourself to? Do you fall into believing that no one has a more accurate view of you than you do? Do you use your knowledge or experience to keep confrontation at bay?

Pastor, you don't have to be afraid of what is in your heart, and you don't have to fear being known, because there is nothing in you that could ever be exposed that hasn't already been covered by the precious blood of your Savior king, Jesus.

CHAPTER TWO

AGAIN AND AGAIN

I wish I could say that my story is unique, that most pastors don't struggle the way that I did. I wish I could say that in the lives of the vast majority of pastors there is no disconnect between their public ministry personas and the details of their private lives. I wish I could say that most pastors are as skilled at preaching the gospel to themselves as they are to others. I wish I could say that relationships between pastors and their staff are seldom tense and seldom break down. I wish I could report that few pastors are angry and bitter. I wish I could tell you that my experience is that most churches pastor their pastors well. I wish I could encourage you with the fact that most pastors are known for their humility and approachability. I wish I could say that most pastors minister out of a deep sense of their own need. Yes, I wish I could say all of these things, but I can't.

Because of what God has called me to do, I am with a different pastoral staff, somewhere in the world, about forty times a year. On these weekends I am obsessively nosy, in the best ministry sense of those words. I love pastors. I love the local church. I understand the push and pull of pastoral ministry. I have experienced its brightest moments and its darkest nights. I know how this calling can seem unbearably burdensome and how it can be a sheer delight. I know pastors not only face trouble but also can be all too skilled at troubling their own trouble. I know no pastor has graduated from his need for forgiving, transforming, empowering, and delivering grace. So I care, and because I care, I want to know what's going on and how the pastor(s) is (are) doing. I love meeting with the pastoral staff and rattling their cages.

I love helping them to communicate what they're going through and how they're doing in the middle of it. I love reminding pastors of the present benefits of the person and work of Jesus. I love helping them to see that their security is not to be found in how much the people of their church will come to love them but in the reality of how much Jesus already has loved them. I love giving the rather proud pastor eyes to see himself with a greater biblical clarity, and I love helping the defeated pastor see himself in light of the grace of the gospel. So I listen carefully. I watch with ministry intent. I draw out stories and probe for their meaning in the heart of the pastor. I try to access the character of the local pastoral/staff culture. I do all of this with one question in mind: how is the gospel of Jesus Christ forming and transforming the heart of this pastor and his local ministry culture?

Besides my commitment to eavesdrop on the life of the pastor and his partners in ministry, there is a second experience that has informed and motivated the material in this book. Almost every weekend I am somewhere teaching on some kind of Christian life topic (marriage, parenting, communication, body of Christ, living in light of eternity, etc.). Again and again on these weekends one of the pastors will pull me into a room and begin to confess to me that he is the "jerk" I have been talking about (I never use that word). He will confess to the sorry state of his marriage, that he is an angry parent, that he numbs himself every evening with too much television, that he deals with ministry pressure by drinking more than he should, or that he has dysfunctional ministry relationships all around him. Here is one of my weekend stories.

The day before I arrived for the weekend I got a call from a senior staff member asking me if I would be willing to spend an hour with the church board. I knew right away what the topic of our conversation was to be. I was ushered into one of the staff offices immediately after the weekend conference was over and was greeted by the shell-shocked board. My heart went out to them before they had shared any of the details of their totally unexpected week. We prayed, and they began to tell their story.

The members of the leadership team had arrived for the weekly Monday morning debrief meeting. Usually they would spend some time in prayer and then talk over the events of Sunday. But this meeting would prove to be different in every way. First, the senior pastor was late. He was never late. He hated being late, but this time he was so late that one of the team members called to see what was wrong and if he was on his way. When he entered the room, they all knew something was wrong, very wrong. He was only forty-five and in the height of his ministry, but he looked old, tired, and beaten. He didn't look like the same man who had preached just a day earlier. He mumbled an apology about being late and without any further hesitation said:

> I'm done, I can't do this anymore. I can't deal with the pressures of ministry. I can't face preaching another sermon. I can't deal with another meeting. If I am honest, I would have to say that all I want to do is leave. I want to leave the ministry, I want to leave this area, and I want to leave my wife. No, there's been no affair. I'm just tired of pretending that I'm someone that I'm not. I'm tired of acting like I'm okay when I'm not. I'm tired of playing as if my marriage is good when it is the polar opposite of good. I can't preach this coming Sunday, and I have to get away alone or I'm going to explode. I'm sorry to lay this on you this way, but I'm done—I can't go on.

And with that, he got up and walked out. The leadership team was too stunned to stop him. After talking amongst themselves and praying together again, they called him and asked him to come back. It was in this following conversation that these fellow leaders came to know a man they had lived and ministered with but had not known.

For me, the attention-getting thing about this sad scenario, which I've heard way too many times, was not its stunning suddenness but the shocking reality that the pastor lived in this day-by-day ministry community fundamentally unknown and uncared for. I helped the leadership team to think about what to do next and how to care for their pastor, but I left with a heavy heart and with the knowledge that they had been cast into something that would be very painful for them all and would not go away very soon.

I have walked through similar scenarios with many pastors all around the world. From Belfast to Los Angeles, from Johannesburg to New York, from Minneapolis to Singapore, from Cleveland to Berlin, I've heard their stories and felt their discouragement, bitterness, aloneness, fear, and longing. As I've told my story, pastors have felt safe in telling their stories. And it has hit me again and again that there are too many pastors with sad stories to tell, and I've wondered again and again to myself, *what's gone wrong with pastoral culture?*

I'm often asked to do material similar to what is in this book as a preconference to a conference on another topic. I always try to be unflinchingly honest while being unshakingly hopeful. I finished addressing about five hundred pastors at one of these preconferences, but I was not prepared for what would happen next. When I finished and came off the platform, a long line of concerned and broken pastors formed in front of me. About five pastors down the line stood a man who wept his way toward me. I think I could have set up a counseling office for two weeks, full-time, and still not have ministered to all the needs that stood before me. It was at this conference that I determined that I would speak to these issues and do all that I could to minister to my fellow pastors. This book is the result of that clear moment of calling.

As I have unpacked my own story and have endeavored to exegete the story of others in ministry, themes have risen to the surface. Yes, each story is unique, and generalizations can be both unhelpful and dangerous, but the pathway to being lost in the middle of your own ministry story is a road that has been traveled by many. Inspecting their journey can help you understand yours.

SIGNS OF A PASTOR LOSING HIS WAY

There are things that my pastor friend, whom I spoke of above, did and did not do that summarize well the signs of a pastor in trouble.

1) HE IGNORED THE CLEAR EVIDENCE OF PROBLEMS.

The evidence was all around him, and yet he simply didn't pay attention. I've noted in other books that no one is more influential in your life than you are, because no one talks to you more than you do. My pastor friend had been in a long conversation with himself denying, minimizing, and rationalizing the evidence that pointed to the fact that he was a man in trouble. No, it wasn't adultery or pornography; his struggle was more fundamental than that. His explosive anger with his children, which was not an irregular experience, was one of those signs. His constant complaints about fellow leaders after ministry meetings was another piece of troubling evidence. The growing distance between him and his wife pictured that something was not right. His nonexistent devotional life pointed to something being wrong. The fact that he numbed himself every night with hours of television pointed to an unsettled heart. His fantasies of ministering in a different capacity or in a different place pointed to something amiss. His skill at giving nonanswers to personal questions was evidence of his losing his way. Yes, there was all kinds of evidence, but it was denied, ignored, or explained away.

This pastor had become what all of us have the tendency in our sin to become—very skilled self-swindlers. Here's how it works. If you aren't daily admitting to yourself that you are a mess and in daily and rather desperate need for forgiving and transforming grace, and if the evidence around has not caused you to abandon your confidence in your own righteousness, then you are going to give yourself to the work of convincing yourself that you are okay. How do you do that? Well, you point to the ample evidence the fallen world gives you, that the people and situations around you are flawed and broken and are, therefore, the reason you respond to life the way you do. You tell yourself again and again that you are not the problem—that it is or they are, but not you. And you tell yourself that you don't really need to change; it's the people and circumstances around you that need to change. What you are doing, although you probably aren't aware of it, is building elaborate, seemingly logical arguments for your own righteousness. Daily you defend it to yourself and find ways to parade it before others. Rather than casting yourself on the mercy of the one true Savior, you are acting as your own savior, building atoning arguments for the rightfulness of what God clearly says is wrong. You deny evidence, defend your righteousness, and resist grace. No wonder things worsen until they finally come to a tipping point. I know this evidence-denying pattern. I got my master's degree in it! The problem was that I was a pastor and I had no sense of the fact that at the very time I was holding the one beautiful Savior before others, I was working hard to be my own savior.

2) HE WAS BLIND TO THE ISSUES OF HIS OWN HEART.

One of the scarier components of remaining sin is its deceitfulness. It is a reality that is vital to acknowledge and confess. Sin blinds. You see, you and I are in possession of two vision systems. There are our physical eyes that enable us to see the physical universe that surrounds us, and there are the eyes of our heart that help us "see" the spiritual realities that are vital to see if we are going to be who we were designed to be and do what we were designed to do. Sin plays havoc with our spiritual vision. Although we are able to see the sin of others with specificity and clarity, we tend to be blind to our own. And the most dangerous aspect of this already dangerous condition is that spiritually blind people tend to be blind to their blindness.

Here's how it works. My pastor friend did his best to hold onto the delusion that no one had a more accurate view of him than he did. He thought no critique of his thoughts, desires, motivations, choices, words, and actions was more reliable than his own. He thought that the only questions and confrontation that he needed were what he brought to himself. He was all too confident in his vision and all too trusting of his critique of himself. When others would question or confront him, without knowing that he was doing it, he would activate his inner lawyer and generate arguments in his own defense. He often told himself that the speaker didn't really know him because if he did, he wouldn't question him in the way that he was. He often angrily said to his wife, "Darling, you just don't know me as well as you think you do."

Because sin blinds, God has set up the body of Christ to function as an instrument of seeing in our lives, so that we can know ourselves with a depth and accuracy that would be impossible if left on our own. But my friend didn't trust the vision help of others; rather, he relied solely on his view of himself and was left to his own blindness. Patterns were left unaddressed, and because they were unaddressed, they were given time and room to grow until the disconnect between his life and ministry became so obvious and burdensome that all he could think of was getting out.

3) HIS MINISTRY LACKED DEVOTION.

I am more and more convinced that what gives a ministry its motivations, perseverance, humility, joy, tenderness, passion, and grace is the devotional life of the one doing ministry. When I daily admit how needy I am, daily meditate on the grace of the Lord Jesus Christ, and daily feed on the restorative wisdom of his Word, I am propelled to share with others the grace that I am daily receiving at the hands of my Savior. There simply is no set of exegetical, homiletical, or leadership skills that can compensate for the absence of this in the life of a pastor. It is my worship that enables me to lead others to worship. It is my sense of need that leads me to tenderly pastor those in need of grace. It is my joy in my identity in Christ that leads me to want to help others live in the middle of what it means to be "in Christ." In fact, one of the things that makes a sermon compelling is that the preacher is worshiping his way through his own sermon.

Having a ministry that is fueled by personal devotion has its roots in humble, heart-deep confession. This is where it all went wrong with my pastor friend and many others in his shoes. Because he denied the evidence that was around him and was blind to his own heart, he tended to see himself as okay, when he wasn't okay. So he wasn't convicted and encouraged by his preparation and didn't sit under his own preaching. His self-satisfaction meant his words and actions in ministry did not grow in the soil of a personal love for and worship of Christ. Preparation became about downloading a body of truths to people who needed to have their thinking rearranged. His counseling was more problem solving than gospel encouraging. And along the way it all began to get dry and unappealing. It quit having life. It all stopped being about worship and became an ever-repeating series of pastoral responsibilities.

4) HE WASN'T PREACHING THE GOSPEL TO HIMSELF.

If you are in ministry and you are not reminding yourself again and again of the *now-ism* of the gospel, that is, the right-here, right-now benefits of the grace of Christ, you will be looking elsewhere to get what can be found only in Jesus. If you are not feeding your soul on the realities of the presence, promises, and provisions of Christ, you will ask the people, situations, and things around you to be the messiah that they can never be. If you are not attaching your identity to the unshakable love of your Savior, you will ask the things in your life to be your Savior, and it will never happen. If you are not requiring yourself to get your deepest sense of well-being vertically, you will shop for it horizontally, and you will always come up empty. If you are not resting in the one true gospel, preaching it to yourself over and over again, you will look to another gospel to meet the needs of your unsettled heart.

Because my pastor friend didn't preach to himself the truths of who he was in Christ, he began to look for rest in places where rest could not be found. In ways he did not realize, he asked the people and situations around him to be his savior. He was all too aware of how his leaders responded to him, and he needed their respect to have inner peace. He needed the congratulatory responses of his congregation to his preaching, because that made him feel good about what he was doing. He had his identity too attached to his opinions and ideas and felt that rejection of them was rejection of him. And as he looked horizontally for what could only be found vertically, he felt more and more alone and under-appreciated. His private conversation with himself was more self-defense, self-pity, and hurt toward others than it was a liberating and motivating rehearsal of the present glories of the love of Christ. Forgetting to preach to himself the gospel he sought to give to others kicked in a downward spiral in his heart, which he was unaware of until it was so burdensome, all he wanted to do was quit.

5) HE WASN'T LISTENING TO THE PEOPLE CLOSEST TO HIM.

In many ways my pastor friend was unknown at the level of the struggles of his heart, but he was not without outside help of any kind. He did live and minister with leaders who cared about him and spoke to him honestly. There were many occasions where a fellow elder or a long-term staffer would approach him about his attitude or about the way he had spoken to someone. There were many times over the years when someone had come to him with concerns about his marriage and the time he was or was not investing there or about things they saw happening in the lives of his children. He had been confronted about how closely he guarded the details of his personal life or about how many late nights he would spend in his office. No, no one knew the momentous war that was being waged in his heart, but he was not left to himself. There was care that, if taken seriously, could have and probably would have got at the bedrock issues of the heart.

Although my friend wasn't overtly dismissive, he didn't really listen. Because he wasn't open, he would tell himself that he had been misunderstood or that things weren't really that bad; he would even say that he was thankful for all the people who cared for him—they just didn't really know all the good things he was doing in his personal life. He was a very approachable guy who was at the same time very skilled at failing to heed the warnings that God was giving him through faithful members of the body of Christ.

6) HIS MINISTRY BECAME BURDENSOME.

This is where it inevitably leads. You've lost sight of the gospel in your personal life; you feel a growing disconnect between your private life and your public ministry persona; your ministry is no longer fueled by your own worship; you feel misunderstood by those around you; you feel wrongly criticized by those in your home; you think that you and your leadership are not treated with the esteem that they deserve; and you are increasingly spiritually empty because you are looking for spiritual life where it cannot be found. The impact of all of these things together is that you find your ministry less and less a privilege and a joy and more and more a burden and a duty.

I think we would be shocked if we knew how many pastors have lost their joy—how many of us get up at the beginning of each week and grind it out, if for no other reason than we don't know what else to do. For how many of us is ministry no longer an act of worship?

How many of us are building a kingdom in our ministries other than the kingdom of God? How many of us are carrying a burden of hurt and bitterness into each ministry moment? How many of us want to escape and just don't know how?

7) HE BEGAN TO LIVE IN SILENCE.

There are two things that kick in here. First, when people are your substitute messiah (you need their respect and support in order to continue), it's hard to be honest with them about your sins, weaknesses, and failures. There is a second thing that kicks in as well: fear. The more separation and discontinuity there is between the real details of my personal life and my public confession and image, the more I will tend to fear being known. I will fear how people would think of and respond to me if they really knew what was going on in my life. I may even fear the loss of my job. So my responses to the concerns and inquiries of others become structured by fear rather than faith. So I do not make the regular, healthy confessions of struggle to my ministry co-partners, I do not ask candidly and humbly for prayer in places where I clearly need it, and I am very careful with how I answer personal questions when they come my way.

This all means that I am no longer benefiting from the insight-giving, protecting, encouraging, warning, preventative, and restoring ministries of the body of Christ. I am trying to do what none of us is able to do—spiritually make it on my own. Autonomous Christianity never works, because our spiritual life was designed by God to be a community project.

8) HE BEGAN TO QUESTION HIS CALLING.

Because I am not seeing myself with accuracy and because ministry has become burdensome, instead of examining my character and my responses, I will tend to begin to question whether I was right in thinking I was called to ministry. You see, there are only two ways to explain the external and internal breakdown of my ministry. Either I am attempting to do something that I was not called to do, or I am thinking and doing the wrong things in the middle of the ministry I was clearly called to. Once you have closed your eyes to the evidence and quit listening to the voices of others, you are left to the blindness and self-righteousness of your yet-sinful heart. This makes it very hard for you to conclude that you are the problem. No, what you will conclude is that ministry or things in your ministry is the problem, and therefore ministry is the thing that needs to be addressed if things are going to change. This is exactly where my pastor friend found himself. He had deep insecurities when it came to his calling that weren't there five years before.

9) HE GAVE WAY TO FANTASIES OF ANOTHER LIFE.

All of these led to one hope, one dream: getting out. At first it scared him to think of such a thing, but he couldn't seem to stop. More and more he got comfortable with the fantasies of doing something else, but he was afraid to speak a word of them to anyone else. Before long, though, he had opened up the subject with his wife, trying to feel her out as to how comfortable she would be with the prospect of life on the other side of ministry, and it wasn't too long before he thought about telling his team he wanted out. It was a bad week that brought it all out in a messier manner than he had envisioned.

I wish I could say that I've seen these dynamics operating only in the heart of this one man, but sadly I can't. I've heard the stories again and again. I can predict what I am going to be told next. And for all the pastors who know they are in trouble, there are many, many who are and don't yet know it. No, not all of these characteristics are in the lives of each of the men I have talked with, but in all of them many of these things are operating. And not only are they operating, but they are operating outside of the motivating, encouraging, empowering, transforming, and delivering truths of the gospel of Jesus Christ. I write this because I am concerned for me and I am concerned for you. And I am concerned for the culture in our churches that allows this to happen, often unchecked.

CHAPTER THREE

BIG THEOLOGICAL BRAINS AND HEART DISEASE

It was a moment of greater insight than I realized at the time. I look back and see it as a sweet moment of divine rescue—just the kind of grace that was to be the passion of the ministry to which I had been called. I was exegeting my way through Romans, Paul's foundational gospel exposition. I had taken a bound legal-sized notebook and cut a square out of the top right-hand corner of every third page so I could glue a page of the Greek text on both sides of the page. I would then fill the pages with corresponding exegetical notes, sermon outlines, and illustrations. It was an exercise that brought all of my recently taught and newly acquired ministry skills together. I found the exercise challenging and exciting. I felt proud that my notebook was filled with my notes on Romans. I was engulfed in an intoxicating world of language syntax and theological argument. I labored over tenses, contexts, objects, and connectors. I studied etymologies and the Pauline vocabulary. I tried to connect every minute detail to the overarching intention of the author. I consulted all of the experts, weighing insight over insight and opinion against opinion. Countless hours of disciplined private study were represented by page upon page of legal-sized page notes. It was all very rewarding.

One evening, hours into exegeting the next section of Romans, it hit me. I had spent hours each day for months studying perhaps the most extensive and gorgeous exposition of the gospel that has ever been written, and I had been fundamentally untouched by its message.

The message had had little impact on me. It had been all grammar and syntax, theological ideas and logical arguments. It had been a massive intellectual exercise but almost completely devoid of spiritual power. I can remember staring at my ink-filled pages. They seemed distant and blurry, somehow not attached to real life, somehow not having anything to do with me. No, I wasn't delusional; I had written all of it, but it all seemed detached from me, my real life, my marriage, my struggles with sin, my past, my future, my deepest hopes, dreams, and fears. I stared at the page, and it seemed impossible that I could have done all of this work when it had been little more than an assignment for a class, for a grade, in pursuit of a degree.

I sat there numb for a moment as if I had been suspended between two worlds, one real and one that seemed anything but real. I thought of all the classes, all the papers, all the tests. I thought of the huge investment of time, energy, and money. Was it all for this? I began to cry—no, I mean really cry. Powerful emotion came out of me, so much so that Luella heard from another room and came in to see if I was okay. I was anything but okay, and she knew it at first glance. Luella bent down, put her arms around me, and asked me to tell her what was wrong. I remember that she looked frightened as she watched her young seminary husband fall apart before her eyes. In my typically dramatic fashion, I told her I was done. That I couldn't continue my seminary studies. I told her it was over.

Fortunately, I am married to a wise and patient woman who helped me get my bearings and stood with me as I continued and then finished my studies. That evening, with my exegetical notebook in my hands, I learned something about myself and about the Scriptures. My eyes began to open to the dangers inherent in academizing our faith. I personally experienced what can happen when the gospel of Jesus Christ gets reduced to a series of theological ideas coupled with all the skills necessary to access those ideas. Bad things happen when maturity is more defined by knowing than it is by being. Danger is afloat when you come to love the ideas more than the God whom they represent and the people they are meant to free.

One of the courses I was asked to teach as a member of the practical theology faculty of Westminster Seminary in Philadelphia was in pastoral counseling. It was the one counseling course that MDiv students who didn't really have any interest in pastoral counseling had to take. It was a required course, and my students took the course only because it was required. I went in each year knowing that my students didn't want to be in the class and didn't have much interest in or commitment to what I was about to teach. I found the first few years of teaching this course to be incredibly difficult until I began to understand the importance of my voice in the lives of these big-brained future pastors. I developed a strategy that not only changed the atmosphere of the course but made me anticipate it each year.

I decided that I would come in each semester armed with a catalog of pastoral horror stories—you know, the kinds of things no pastor really wants to deal with but which all pastors do. I told my students stories of the late-night calls from wives who have just been slugged by their husbands, of the grief of the mother who has discovered her fifteen-year-old daughter is pregnant, of standing with a mom and dad before the casket of their four-year-old son, of the hours with the severely depressed person or with the man who has spent his family into financial disaster. I told them stories of the grief and travail of the body of Christ as it is lived with the realities of life in a sin-broken world. I told stories of fear, disloyalty, discouragement, anger, depression, aloneness, and loss. I wanted my students to understand that they are called not just to preach exegetically correct and theologically precise sermons but also to pastor people, to walk, live, support, and suffer with them. I wanted them to know that they are called to be more than local-church theological instructors; they are called to be Christ's ambassadors, to be the look on his face, the touch of his hand, and the tone of his voice. I wanted them to feel the weight of being called to make an invisible Christ visible in the lives of people who desperately need to "see" his presence and remember his grace. I longed for them to understand that they aren't called just to *teach* theology to their people but also to *do* theology with their people. I wanted them to grapple with the question of whether they were in seminary because they loved the labyrinthine superstructure of the theological concepts of Scripture or because they loved Jesus and wanted to be his tool of transformation in the lives of messy people.

I began each semester by dipping into stories of my own pastoral unreadiness and failure, with hopes that my narrative would be used to birth in them a greater, more roundly biblical vision of pastoral ministry. It was in the middle of one of those stories when something happened that I will never forget, nor will any of the students who were in that class. I was recounting my own heart struggle, when I had been asked yet again to visit a man who had already eaten up much of my pastoral time and energy, when one of my students raised his hand and blurted out, "All right, Professor Tripp, we know that we will have these projects in our churches. Tell us what to do with them so we can get back to the work of the ministry!" There are many things to pay attention to in his statement, but notice this: he didn't even call the struggling people, to whom we are all called to bring the gospel, "people." To him they were *projects*, that is, obstructions in the way of his definition of ministry. Now, if these people are not the focus and object of ministry, then what is ministry? There was no love for people in this student's statement, and if there was no love for people in his vision of ministry, then it is safe to conclude that there was little operational love for Christ either. He was like many other idea, technology-of-theology guys who populated so many of my classes. My rather pejorative term for them was *theologeeks*, the guys who see theology as an end in itself rather than as a means to an end. They love the academy and would unwittingly drag the academy into the local church and preach sermons that are more theological lectures than gospel meditations.

I walked down the aisle to his desk, knelt down so we were face-to-face, and asked him to repeat what he had said, loudly and word for word. I was pastoring him at the moment and the class who had heard what he had said. I wanted them never to forget that moment. I asked him to repeat what he had called these people. He softly said,

"Projects." It was a wonderful, God-given teaching moment. Not too long ago I was greeted by a pastor who had been in that class years before. He had remembered it and had been warned again and again by his memory.

Over the years of teaching this course many of my students asked if I would counsel them. Here's what the dynamic was: as I talked to them about the *now-ism* of the gospel and encouraged them with the power of the gospel to transform lives in very concrete ways, students in the class would reflect on issues in their own lives. Since the class would uncover things that had not been previously uncovered, and since they were just a few months from graduating and stepping into some kind of ministry position, they felt the urgency to deal with what the course had exposed. I was unprepared for the narratives that I would hear and the kinds of things my students were struggling with.

Frank was one of the first. He had been married for fifteen years, had four children from young teenager on down, and had come to seminary after a successful career in finance. We sat down in my office, and after way too much small talk it became obvious that Frank was having trouble talking about what had motivated him to seek my help. I reassured him of my commitment to him, the importance of his getting help, and the confidentiality of our relationship. What he blurted out next I was unprepared for: "I have a closet of women's clothes in my basement that I put on at night; it's the one time in my day when I feel comfortable." I must admit I was a bit blown away. He was a very bright and gifted young theologian, an intellectual star of sorts. He lived and worked with the Word of God every day. He could parse the details of the gospel of Jesus Christ. Yet with all of this he was lost in a world of deep identity confusion, and the gospel that he was studying in order to help others seemed unable to rescue him. I wondered what he was telling himself as he did ministry interviews. I wondered how his wife had made her way through all of this. I wondered how he thought he'd be able to keep it from his increasingly sophisticated children. But most of all, I wondered how you wear women's clothes at night and get up the next morning and exegete Colossians.

George didn't find it as hard to talk to me, because he was no longer able to trust himself, and he was scared. He had begun to study at Barnes and Noble at night after dinner with his wife. He found it gave him a break from the hothouse of seminary while providing a quiet place to study. It wasn't long before he began to notice all the beautiful young women who also chose Barnes and Noble as their evening hangout. One night he sighted a beautiful young lady and actually moved in order to position himself to have a better, more strategic look at her. Sometimes he would sit so that he could have eye contact with one of these ladies, or he would sit so that he could have the view of them that he wanted without their feeling his stare. Some months in, he saw the woman he was watching get up and leave, so he did the same, perhaps hoping they would bump into one another. She got into her car without noticing him, and he went back in to study. This led to not merely leaving when a woman left but getting in his car and following her, at a distance, to her home. He asked to see me the night after he had followed a woman all the way home, got out of his car, and walked up to her door. Just before he knocked, he got scared and ran to his car and drove away. In class he seemed to be a sweet and pliable seminary student; the contrast between the day and night of his life was stunning.

I was told stories of nearly broken marriages, of domestic violence, of women who were ready to walk out, of angry men, of broken relationships with children and extended families, of private sexual sin, of conflict with neighbors and in church, of deep debt, of battles with depression and anxiety, of obsessive and compulsive thoughts, and of Internet pornography.

The more I heard, the more I was convinced that the things I was being exposed to in the lives of my students were not just individual; they were systemic. I determined I was going to pastor my students; I would apply whatever I was teaching to the foundational thoughts and motives of their hearts. I became convinced that it is dangerous to handle Scripture any other way. Yet when I would endeavor to do so, I would often get push-back from one of my students. One student even confronted me in front of the whole class, saying, "Professor Tripp, you're preaching at us. This is a seminary classroom, which means this is not your church, and we are not your congregation." Yes, it really did happen.

Over the years I had heard way too much "Will we need to know this for the exam?" and not enough "Help me understand how to live in light of what you are now teaching us." I have received many arrogant and self-assured response papers from students who saw themselves as more my teacher than my student. I would read and shudder to think that they were going to be someone's pastor very soon. Were all of my students in some kind of personal spiritual trouble? Of course not, but many were, and most of them had no idea, even though they were looking in the mirror of the Word of God every day. This sad experience has been a major motivator for writing this book. It has led me to meditate upon and discuss with others this question: what is wrong with the way that we seek to prepare people for local church ministry?

WHAT ARE WE DOING WITH THE WORD?

I have a friend (about whom I have written before) who became an avid rose gardener. His rose garden was the community's most beautiful and healthy and with the widest variety of roses. He did everything humanly possible to prune, protect, and nourish his bushes into maximum health and productivity. During the season, he would work many hours every day on his bushes. He did it with discipline and perseverance. He told himself he did it because he loved roses. He didn't mind the early mornings or the gardening that repeatedly took him into the night. His wife thought he was a little nuts, and his friends wondered what it was about roses that hooked this guy, but nothing seemed to weaken his resolve. He knew the URL of all of the important rosebush sites, he was friends with all the good nursery proprietors in his area, and he had filled his head with endless trivia about the history, health, and care of roses. He was able to speak in a rose lingo that needed translation if the listener was not himself a "roser."

One Friday evening after three hours of rose work, he was looking out the window as he washed his hands at the kitchen sink, and it struck him all of a sudden that the one thing he hadn't done in years with his roses was enjoy them. He had studied the world of roses. He had cultivated the soil around his rose bushes. He had carefully pruned his bushes. He had given bunches of roses to others. He had fed and watered his roses. He had had long discussions with other rosers. He had spent time at the local nurseries learning more and examining bay bushes with the intent to purchase. But with all of the time invested in roses, he hadn't taken the time to enjoy the fruits of his labor. He had become an expert, but he had not been moved or changed by the display of beauty that was the object of all his efforts.

That evening, as he stood at his sink, he determined he would do what he hadn't taken time to do: he would enjoy his roses. The next morning he decided to get up and go out and sit in his rose garden—sit in front of one of the objects of his work—but this time he wouldn't work; he would sit, watch, listen, and enjoy. So before noon, he placed himself in front of one of his bushes, and for hours he just sat there. He noticed how every branch of each bush was unique. He noticed the individual curvature and placement of each thorn. He watched the insect civilization that attached itself to each bush. He noticed the contrast between the new-growth green of the infant shoots and the rough-bark exterior of the older branches of the bush. He was awestruck by the precise and delicate architecture of each blossom. He couldn't believe how each yellow petal wasn't really one shade of yellow but actually a wash of a hundred different yellow hues coursing across it that gave it its yellow appearance. He told me that it may seem weird to say, but his hours before that bush changed him. Those hours gave him back his sight; they made him thankful, they made him smile at the level of his heart, they filled him with mystery and joy, and, most importantly, they caused him to worship.

You see, those bushes were never intended to be an end in themselves. No, those bushes were designed to be a means to an end. The glory of the bushes isn't ultimate glory. No, it's *sign* glory, like every other created thing. All creation is meant to be a finger pointing us to ultimate glory, the only glory that can ever satisfy the human heart, the glory of God. My friend was a rose expert, but he had seen neither the sign nor what the sign pointed to. Expert, but unchanged. Expert, but without awe. Expert, but not driven to worship. Expert, but lacking in joy. Expert, but not very thankful. It was a sad state of affairs for a man who professed to love roses.

Could it be that this is very close to what a seminary education might do to its students? Is it not possible for seminary students to become experts in a gospel that they are not being exposed and changed by? Is it not dangerous to teach students to be comfortable with the radical content of Scripture while holding it separate from their hearts and lives? Is it not dangerous for students to become comfortable with the message of the Bible while not being broken, grieved, and convicted by it? Is it not important for seminary students to be faced daily with the personal implications of the message that they're learning to unpack and deliver to others? Is it not vital to hold before students who are investigating the theology of Christ the frequent and consistent call to life-shaping love for Christ? Could it be that many students in seminary are too academically busy to sit before the Rose of Sharon in awe, love, and worship? Could it be that in academizing the faith, we have unwittingly made the means to an end the end? Shouldn't every Christian institution of higher learning be a warm, nurturing, Christ-centered, gospel-driven community of faith? Could it be that rather than having as our mission students who have mastered the Book, our goal should be graduating students who have been mastered by the God of the Book?

Isaiah 55, one of the Bible's most beautiful offers of grace, confronts us right at this point:

> For as the rain and the snow come down from heaven
>   and do not return there but water the earth,
> making it bring forth and sprout,
>   giving seed to the sower and bread to the eater,
> so shall my word be that goes out from my mouth;
>   it shall not return to me empty,

but it shall accomplish that which I purpose,
    and shall succeed in the thing for which I sent it.
For you shall go out in joy
    and be led forth in peace;
the mountains and the hills before you
    shall break forth into singing,
    and all the trees of the field shall clap their hands.
Instead of the thorn shall come up the cypress;
    instead of the brier shall come up the myrtle;
and it shall make a name for the LORD,
    an everlasting sign that shall not be cut off. (vv. 10–13)

I have heard many sermons preached out of the first stanza of this great promise. It is very encouraging that God's Word will not return empty. It is very motivating to know that God's words always accomplish God's purpose. It is wonderful to understand that I do not have to worry about results and outcomes. It is good to know that the God of the Word has a purpose for his Word and that he stands behind his Word, securing its productivity. All of this is amazing and stimulating, but I am always left as a bit of a crazy man when I hear a preacher expound this declaration without unpacking the critical question that it leaves. Declaring that God's Word will always accomplish its purpose leaves you with this inescapable question: what, then, is its purpose? You simply cannot understand the genius and hope of this passage without answering this question. You see, it is quite possible and, sadly, quite regular for us to use the Bible unbiblically. Even given its God-driven purposefulness, you can approach, handle, and make use of the Word of God in ways that are outside of its intended purpose.

The second stanza of this passage answers the question that the first asks. In beautiful, nature-oriented word pictures, it calls us to recognize that the ultimate purpose for the Word is worship. This has to be so, because the deep drama of this broken world and the image bearers that inhabit it is a drama of worship. The gospel narrative is all about the larceny and restoration of true worship, the thing for which we were given breath, the worship of God. The story that the

Word of God contains guarantees a time when all of creation will bow in worship of God. All sin is idolatrous, and grace's work is to reclaim the deepest desires, passions, thoughts, and motives of our heart for God. This confronts us with the fact that the content and theology of the Word of God is not an end in itself but must be viewed as a means to an end. The intended end of this content is God-honoring, life-shaping worship.

But there are more left wondering, "How is this heart-deep worship produced?" This is where the passage goes next. It employs one of the stranger word pictures in the Bible. Remember, the overarching metaphor is the falling of rain and snow. Strangely, this passage says that when this rain falls down, the thornbush will become a cypress and the brier will become a myrtle. Now think with me. If you have a little thornbush in your backyard and it's nourished by the snow and rain, what do you expect to get? The obvious answer is a bigger thornbush. If the rain and snow water that brier in your yard, you know the result will be a bigger brier. But not so with the Word of God; when this rain falls on the thornbush it actually becomes something organically different! The picture here is of fundamental, specific, and personal transformation.

When the Word of God, faithfully taught by the people of God and empowered by the Spirit of God, falls down, people become different. Lusting people become pure, fearful people become courageous, thieves become givers, demanding people become servants, angry people become peacemakers, complainers become thankful, and idolaters come to joyfully worship the one true God. The ultimate purpose of the Word of God is not theological information but heart and life transformation. Biblical literacy and theological expertise are not, therefore, the end of the Word but a God-ordained means to an end, and the end is a radically transformed life because the worship at the center of that life has been reclaimed. This means it is dangerous to teach, discuss, and exegete the Word without this goal in view. It should be the goal of every seminary professor. It should be his prayer for every one of his students. It should cause him or her to make regular pastoral pleas to the students. It means recognizing that this student's future ministry will never be shaped by his knowledge and skill alone but also, inevitably, by the condition of his heart.

Think about it. When a pastor has left his office and is at home yelling at his wife, he's not ignorant of the fact that his yelling is wrong. At that point he doesn't care what is right or wrong, because something else is ruling his heart. When a pastor is responding to issues in his church in ways that are more political than pastoral, it's not because he's ignorant of the selfishness of this response but because he's more committed to building his kingdom than God's. When a pastor is eaten with envy over the ministry position of another, he isn't giving way to envy out of ignorance of its danger but because his self-absorbed heart feels entitled to what is a blessing and not a right.

Have we accomplished our training task if we produce generations of graduates who have big theological brains but tragically diseased hearts? Must we not hold together theological training and personal transformation? Should we not require every seminary classroom to be faithful to God's intended purpose for his Word? Shouldn't every seminary professor have pastoral love for his students? Shouldn't every instructor long to be used of God to produce a growing love for Christ in each of his students?

I am convinced that the crisis of pastoral culture often begins in the seminary class. It begins with a distant, impersonal, information-based handling of the Word of God. It begins with pastors who, in their seminary years, became quite comfortable with holding God's Word distant from their own hearts. It begins with classrooms that are academic without being pastoral. It begins with brains becoming more important than hearts. It begins with test scores being more important than character. The problem with all of these things is that they're subtle and deceptive. They don't exist in a black-or-white world of either/or but in a messy world of both/and. Yes, every seminary professor would say that he cares about the hearts of his students. All of us would say that we want to stimulate love for Christ.

The question is, does this goal shape the content and process of the theological education to which we have given ourselves?

THE SPECIALIZATION OF THEOLOGICAL EDUCATION

If you would go back, let's say, a hundred years, every professor in the classroom would be a churchman. He would have come to theological education by means of the pastorate. In these men there burned a love for the local church. They came to the classroom carrying the humility and wisdom gained only by their years in the trenches. They taught with the hearts and lives of real people in view—the people with whom they had wept, become angry, rejoiced, and contended. They came to the classroom knowing that the biggest battles of pastoral ministry were fought on the turf of their own hearts. They were pastors who were called not to quit pastoring but to bring pastoral love and zeal into the ecosystem of theological education.

But over the years theological education began to change. It became more specialized and more departmentalized. Over the years more and more professors came to the seminary classroom with little or no local church experience. They got to the classroom not because they were successful pastors and therefore equipped to train and disciple the next generation. No, they got to the seminary classroom because they were experts in their field. So the energy in the classroom was not cloning a new generation of pastors but cloning experts in apologetics, ethics, systematics, church history, and biblical languages. It has been a subtle but seismic change in the culture of the seminary and the kind of results it produces. In some situations it all degenerates into a culture of little feudal kingdoms (the kingdom of systematics or ethics, etc.) with the professor as the feudal lord, guarding the kingdom he has built and protecting the turf he has acquired against the expansion of other kingdoms. The student matriculates from kingdom to kingdom, always being assured that the particular kingdom of his present focus is the most vital to the health of the federation of kingdoms that makes up the world of theological education. It is a politically charged culture, more given to gate keeping than to pastoring and more focused on vital information acquisition than on character development. I write these things as a pastor with a heavy heart who lived in this culture for twenty years. I know what I have written will make some angry, and I know that the system has a way of rising to defend itself, but it's a price I am willing to pay. The stakes are that high. Seminary self-examination is that important. Honest talk is vital.

SO WHAT'S THE DANGER?

Academized Christianity, which is not constantly connected to the heart and puts its hope in knowledge and skill, can actually make students dangerous. It arms them with powerful knowledge and skills that can make the students think that they are more mature and godly than they actually are. It arms students with weapons of spiritual warfare that if not used with humility and grace will harm the people they are meant to help.

Permit me to list the things that may happen in the lives of the students when the seminary environment is less than faithful to God's intention for his Word. I will write just a couple sentences about each.

1) SPIRITUAL BLINDNESS

Because sin blinds, and those blinded by sin tend to be blind to their blindness, it is dangerous to handle the truths of the Word without asking students to look into the mirror of the Word and see themselves as they actually are. Students who don't do this will enter ministry convinced that they are prepared to fix the world but will fail to recognize that they need fixing just as much as anyone to whom they have been called to minister.

2) THEOLOGICAL SELF-RIGHTEOUSNESS

For students who have not been required to confess that it is easier to learn theology than to live it, it is tempting to think maturity is more a matter of knowing than a matter of living. They think that godliness is more a matter of what you intellectually grasp then a matter of how you live your life. So, puffed up with knowledge, they smugly think they are okay.

3) DYSFUNCTIONAL PERSONAL RELATIONSHIP TO THE WORD

Somewhere in his theological education, the student loses his devotional relationship not only to the Word but also to the God of the Word. Study of the Word becomes more a world of correct ideas than a world of submission to the Lord, whom those ideas introduce and define.

4) LACK OF PERSONAL GOSPEL NEEDINESS

Since the student has come to think of himself as more mature than he actually is because of the knowledge he has gained, he doesn't approach God's Word with a tenderness and neediness of heart. His study of the Word brings him again and again to his desk, but it seldom brings him to his knees.

5) IMPATIENCE WITH OTHERS

I have written and said many times that no one gives grace better than the person who is deeply persuaded that he needs it himself. Self-righteous people tend to be critical, dismissive, and impatient with others.

6) WRONG PERSPECTIVE ON MINISTRY

Because of all this, ministry is driven more by theological correctness than by worship of and love for the Lord Jesus Christ. The sermon becomes more of a theological lecture than an exposition of the grace of the gospel and a plea to run after the Savior. Sadly, it is often driven more by the passion for ideas than by love for people and for Christ.

7) NO LIVING COMMUNION WITH CHRIST

It can finally all degenerate into a Christ-less Christianity that puts its hope in theology and rules and somehow forgets that if theology and rules had the power to transform the heart of idolaters, Jesus would never have had to come, live, die, and rise again. It ends with the means becoming the end and a Christianity devoid of power against the world, the flesh, and the Devil.

WHERE DO WE GO FROM HERE?

I am not suggesting at all that the seminary curriculum needs to be gutted. All the areas of study that make up seminary education are vital. What I am suggesting is that pastoral passion for the students shape the way the content of seminary education is delivered and applied. I am suggesting that seminary professors become committed to making community with their students and that they always teach with the heart in view and the transforming power of the gospel as their hope. I am suggesting that the seminary student should feel known and loved by his professors and that, in the process of his education, he will come to know his heart and his Lord more deeply and more fully. I am suggesting that seminary classrooms should be places of both education and worship. I am suggesting that professors must preach to and pastor their students. I am suggesting that spiritual formation is not a department of theological education or a particular course. No, the goal of spiritual formation must dye the content of every area of study. Finally I am suggesting that every course of study hold before each student a beautiful Savior, whose beauty alone has the power to overwhelm any other beauty that could capture his heart.

CHAPTER FOUR

MORE THAN KNOWLEDGE AND SKILL

I have heard the tale again and again. The summary is always the same: "We finally came to the realization that we had called (hired) someone we didn't know." The most recent story was quite typical. The senior pastor, now in his sixties, knows his time to step down is drawing near. A search committee is formed and begins to develop the criteria they will use for vetting the applicants. The opening is published through the church's network, and the process begins. Other than a few lines that were vague and all too general, the two pages describing the profile of the man they were looking for showed little interest in the man himself. Getting to know the heart of the man, whose impressive list of knowledge and skills was expected to jump off the application page, was simply not a part of the search process in an essential way.

There was excitement at the search committee meeting when the head of the committee presented the application of the man that seemed to fit their profile in every way. Not only did he have the right training, the right skill set, and what seemed to be the right ministry philosophy for bonding with and growing their church, but also he came with a resume of ministry experience in a variety of settings. By the end of the meeting the search group had decided to send a delegation to hear the man preach and get a read of how his current church was doing. After hearing him speak that first Sunday morning, it was full steam ahead for the committee. They loved the way he handled the passage, and several members of the committee remarked that his preaching reminded them of their retiring pastor. It wasn't long before he was invited to preach at the calling church, followed by a Monday morning interview and an invitation later that week to be the new senior pastor of the church. Yes, there were cursory interviews with elders and deacons, and the group had one opportunity to meet his family, but the reality is that once he matched their profile of knowledge, experience, and skill, it was hard for the committee to listen to or hear anything that would get in the way of offering him a call.

The first several months of his ministry at this new church were filled with enthusiasm and hope. It did seem as though God had provided just the right person. There was one thing that gave some insightful people pause: the new pastor's wife seemed neither comfortable nor happy. She was not bonding with the ladies of the church, and she seemed to participate only in the required "pastor's-wife-must-be-there" activities. He was not around the office as much as the staff had anticipated and was therefore hard to reach, but these seemed to be minor issues. "Eight months, and no one has been invited to their house or spent time with them socially," was the concerned comment of a wise, old elder as he met for coffee with a fellow leader. It was clear that the new pastor hated meetings and was socially uncomfortable in informal settings. He spent most of his time during the week studying at his home office and generally only showed up at the church for Thursday staff meetings and Sunday services. The staff had to learn how to operate without him, and the interns felt abandoned. In public settings he seemed like the quintessential qualified and experienced pastor, but the public persona and the private man were beginning to collide, and no one seemed to know.

At the end of the first year, he announced that his wife was going home for a time to be with her parents. He said he felt that it was too soon for him to take time off, so she and the kids would be gone for a couple weeks, and he would be "batching it" on his own. No one thought much about it, and meals were provided so that he would not starve in his wife's absence. It made people wonder when two weeks stretched to four, but not many questions were asked. It wasn't long after his wife returned that he began to ask for prayer for his family and for the "normal" tensions that pastors experience between family and ministry. Meanwhile his wife did not appear to be any better adjusted to her new ministry home or any closer to her peer group in the church.

His abnormal isolation from the staff and leadership of the church and his wife's abnormal discomfort with her new church community became the new normal. Everyone seemed to adjust and to forget what had been and what could be. The staff learned to load all their essential dealing with the senior pastor onto Thursdays, the interns learned to make their own way, and the congregation seemed content with well-functioning public gatherings. The "less-than-what-should-be" became the "we-can-make-this-work." This is often the way it is.

I'm convinced that the big crisis for the church of Jesus Christ is not that we are easily dissatisfied but that we are all too easily satisfied. We have a regular and perverse ability to make things work that are not and should not be working. We learn to adjust to things that we should alter. We learn to be okay with things we should be confronting. We learn how to avoid things we should be facing. We would rather be comfortable than to hold people accountable. We swindle ourselves into thinking that things are better than they are, and in so doing we compromise the calling and standards of the God we say we love and serve. Like sick people who are afraid of the doctor, we collect evidence that points to our health when really, in our heart of hearts, we know we are sick. So we settle for a human second best, when God, in grace, offers us so much more.

Four years in, and the evidence was mounting and inescapable that something was wrong in the heart and life of this man and his family. He often looked beaten and distracted. He had become less patient and more easily irritated with those who worked with him, and his wife often looked as if she was at the edge of tears. He quietly asked the deacons if there was a fund that could assist in getting counseling for him and his wife, and money was gladly provided.

People in the inner circle were heartened by the fact that the couple was seeking help and, looking back months later, were thankful that a crisis had been avoided. But it hadn't.

The call that no elder wants to get came to the head of the elder board on a cold winter Saturday afternoon. It was the pastor asking if there was any possibility of finding someone to fill in for him the next day (two morning sermons and a missions luncheon talk). The elder mistakenly thought his pastor must be physically sick, so when the pastor told him it was a family emergency, his heart sank. Little did he know what the next few days would bring.

Monday the pastor called an emergency meeting of the executive committee of the board and told them what was going on. On Saturday the pastor's wife had given him an ultimatum: "It's me or your ministry. You have to choose one or the other, because you're not going to have both." She went on to say that she could not do it anymore. She couldn't deal with the huge disconnect between their public and private lives. She said she was exhausted with pretending that things were okay when they were everything but okay. She was tired of hearing her husband consistently call people to do things he wasn't doing. She hated the new city she lived in and bitterly reminded her husband that she had begged him not to uproot her and the children. Having unloaded on him, she then told him that she would not be in church on Sunday or any other Sunday to come. It was "done, over" and he would have to make her and the children the focus of his attention "for the first time in many years."

"She's right," he said with head bowed. "It has gone on too long. I don't know if this is my resignation, a request for a leave of absence, or just a cry for help, but we can't continue doing what we have been doing. My wife is home packing. She's heading with the kids to her mother's, and I plan to go as well, as soon as this meeting is over and I have put several ministry things in order." The shocked executive committee should not have been shocked. They should have known. They should have guided, counseled, and protected. They should have warned and encouraged. They should have served and rescued.

But they had hired a man they did not know in a marriage they did not know and with a wife who was more troubled than they knew. They were persuaded by a body of knowledge, the history of ministry experience, and obvious ministry skills. They made assumptions they should not have made. They failed to ask questions that they should have asked. They knew the vitae of the man, but they did not know his heart. Had they known, they never would have called him, because they would have been able to predict what they were now dealing with.

They had no knowledge of the late-night arguments between their potential pastor and his wife that had led up to his acceptance of the call. They did not know that the isolation the staff and interns had been experiencing was also the experience of every member of the pastor's family. They did not know that the reason he had sought and taken this new position was that his relationship with his wife had already begun to disintegrate, and she was already beginning to emotionally crash. They did not know that she had been devastated when he took the call and that he was convinced it was the only way to rescue his marriage and family. The operative words that unpack the crisis of this one local church and many other churches that are going through similar things are "they did not know."

WHAT MAKES PASTORS SUCCESSFUL?

I am convinced that much of the problem in situations like this is an unbiblical definition of the essential ingredients of ministry success. Sure, on their candidate profile was a line that required, "Vibrant walk with the Lord," but these words were weakened by a process that asked few questions in this area while making grand assumptions. They were really interested in his knowledge (right theology), skill (good preacher), ministry philosophy (will build the church), and experience (isn't cutting his pastoral teeth in our place of ministry). Because of what I do, many times I have heard church leaders, in moments of pastoral crisis, say to me, "We didn't know the man we hired."

What does knowing the man mean? It means knowing the true condition of his heart (as far as that is possible). What does he really love, and what does he despise? What are his hopes, dreams, and fears? What are the deep desires that fuel and shape the way he does ministry? What are the anxieties that have the potential to derail or paralyze him? How accurate is his view of himself? Is he open to the confrontation, critique, and encouragement of others? Is he committed to his own sanctification? Is he open about his own temptations, weaknesses, and failures? Is he ready to listen to and defer to the wisdom of others? Does he see pastoral ministry as a community project? Does he have a tender, nurturing heart? Is he warm and hospitable, a shepherd and champion to those who are suffering? What character qualities would his wife and children use to describe him? Does he sit under his own preaching? Is his heart broken and his conscience regularly grieved as he looks at himself in the mirror of the Word? How robust, consistent, joyful, and vibrant is his devotional life? Does his ministry to others flow out of the vibrancy of his devotional communion with the Lord? Does he hold himself to high standards, or is he willing to give way to mediocrity? Is he sensitive to the experiences and needs of those who minister alongside of him? Is he one who incarnates the love and grace of the Redeemer? Does he overlook minor offenses? Is he ready and willing to forgive? Is he critical and judgmental? Is the public pastor a different person from the private husband and dad? Does he take care of his physical self? Does he numb himself with too much social media or television? If he said, "If only I had _________," what would fill in the blank? How successful has he been in pastoring the congregation that is his family?

You see, it is absolutely vital to remember that a pastor's ministry is never just shaped by his knowledge, experience, and skill. It is always also shaped by the true condition of his heart. In fact, if his heart is not in the right place, all of the knowledge and skill can actually function to make him dangerous. Let's examine the situation that I have been unpacking for you.

The problem was not the pastor's wife, although she had significant heart issues to deal with. The problem was not that he had a perennially troubled marriage. The problem was not his isolation from ministry partners and the body of Christ. All of these things were the signs and symptoms of a deeper, more foundational problem. The problem was one of the heart, one that would have an inescapable negative effect on his ministry. The problem was a vertical problem. It had to do with the character and content of this pastor's relationship with God.

The problem was the pastor's lack of a living, humble, needy, celebratory, worshipful, meditative communion with Christ. It was as if Jesus had left the building. There were all kinds of ministry knowledge and skill, but those seemed divorced from a living communion with a living and ever-present Christ. All this knowledge, skill, and activity seemed to be fueled by something other than love for Christ and a deep, abiding gratitude for the love of Christ. In fact, it was all shockingly impersonal. It was about theological content, exegetical rightness, ecclesiastical commitments, and institutional advancement. It was about preparing for the next sermon, getting the next meeting agenda straight, and filling the requisite leadership openings. It was about budgets, strategic plans, and ministry partnerships. None of these things are wrong in themselves. Many of them are essential. But they must never be ends in themselves. They must never be the engine that propels the vehicle. They must all be an expression of something deeper, and that something deeper must reside in the heart of the senior pastor. It must ignite and fuel his ministry at every level, and what ignites his ministry must ignite every aspect of his personal life as well.

The pastor must be enthralled by, in awe of—can I say it: in love with—his Redeemer so that everything he thinks, desires, chooses, decides, says, and does is propelled by love for Christ and the security of rest in the love of Christ. He must be regularly exposed, humbled, assured, and given rest by the grace of his Redeemer. His heart needs to be tenderized day after day by his communion with Christ so that he becomes a tender, loving, patient, forgiving, encouraging, and giving servant leader. His meditation on Christ—his presence, his promises, and his provisions—must not be overwhelmed by his meditation on how to make his ministry work.

You see, it is only love for Christ that can defend the heart of the pastor against all the other loves that have the potential to kidnap his ministry. It is only worship of Christ that has the power to protect him from all the seductive idols of ministry that will whisper in his ear. It is only the glory of the risen Christ that will guard him against the self-glory that is a temptation to all who are in ministry and that destroys the ministry of so many. Only Christ can turn an arrogant, "bring on the world" seminary graduate into a patient, humble giver of grace. Only deep gratitude for a suffering Savior can make a man willing to suffer in ministry. It is only a heart that is satisfied in Christ that can be spiritually content in the hardships of ministry. It is only in your brokenness in the face of your sin that you can give grace to the fellow rebels to whom God has called you to minister. It's only when your identity is firmly rooted in Christ that you are free from seeking to get your identity out of your ministry.

We must be careful how we define ministry readiness and spiritual maturity. There is a danger of thinking that the well-educated and trained seminary graduate is ministry ready or to mistake ministry knowledge, busyness, and skill with personal spiritual maturity. Maturity is a vertical thing that will have a wide variety of horizontal expressions. Maturity is about relationship to God that results in wise and humble living. Maturity of love for Christ expresses itself in love for others. Thankfulness for the grace of Christ expresses itself in grace to others. Gratitude for the patience and forgiveness of Christ enables you to be patient and forgiving toward others. It is your own daily experience of the rescue of the gospel that gives you a passion for people to experience the same rescue.

Because all of this is true, these things need to be brought to the forefront in the application and examination of all pastoral candidates. We are not calling skills, knowledge, and experience to ministry. We are calling whole people who live out of the heart and whose ministries will always be shaped and directed by some kind of worship. We are calling people in the middle of their own sanctification, still struggling with the seductive and deceptive power of sin. We are calling people who face the daily snares of a world that is simply not operating the way that God intended. We are calling people whom God will call into hardship for their redemptive good and for his glory. We are calling people who are in intimate daily relationships with other sinners. We are calling people who are capable of losing their way, capable of self-deception, and tempted to be self-sufficient and self-righteous. We are calling people who drag their feelings about and interpretations of previous ministry experiences into this new place of ministry. We are calling people who are as desperately in need of forgiving, transforming, empowering, and delivering grace as anybody to whom they would ever minister. We are calling people, real people who are not yet grace graduates.

So we must get to know, really know, the people we put into positions of spiritual leadership and care of God's people.

SOME BIBLICAL EXAMPLES

It is clear from examining Scripture that leadership fruitfulness or failure is seldom only about knowledge, strategy, skill, and experience. Consider what is said of Abraham in Romans 4. He was chosen by God to receive his covenant promises. He was told that his offspring would be like the sand on the seashore. Yet his wife was a very old woman, way, way beyond childbearing age, and he had not yet given birth to the son who would carry on his line. Romans 4 tells us something very significant about Abraham's heart. Think about it: when you and I are called by God to wait for an extended period as Abraham was, often for us our story of waiting is a chronicle of ever-weakening faith. The longer we have time to think about what we are waiting for, the longer we have time to consider how we have no ability to deliver it; and the longer we have to let ourselves wonder why we have been selected to wait, the more our faith weakens. But not so with Abraham. We're told in this passage that during this time of protracted waiting, his faith actually grew stronger, and the passage tells us why. Rather than meditating on the impossibility of his situation, Abraham meditated on the power and the character of the One who had made the promise. The more Abraham let his heart bask in the glory of God, the more convinced he became that he was in good hands. Rather than a cycle of discouragement and hopelessness, Abraham's story was one of encouragement and hope. Why? Because he meditated on the right thing.

What about Joseph, whom God had chosen as his tool to preserve the children of Israel from famine and resultant extinction? When seduced by the Egyptian ruler Potiphar's wife, he would not give in. Why? It wasn't fear of consequences, or what he had learned from past experiences, or his skill at negotiating the complicated relationships of the palace. Genesis 39 tells us clearly what motivated Joseph at this critical-choice point in his life. You see, he was able to resist because of the deep heart devotion he had to his Lord. His heart was not ruled by horizontal pleasure but by vertical worship. He could not conceive of doing such a wicked thing against God. A glory greater than the temporary glories of the created world had captured his heart; and so he spoke with an immediate, emphatic, and heartfelt no.

Or think about Moses as he stands before that burning bush. God had chosen Moses to be his tool of redemption, to lead Israel out of captivity and into the land of promise. But Moses is neither willing nor hopeful. Exodus 3 and 4 record Moses's argument with God. Moses's personal assessment is that he is completely unable, unprepared, and unqualified to do the thing that God has called him to do. God's response is simple: "I will go with you." Moses's bottom line is just as simple: "Oh, my Lord, please send someone else" (4:13). Moses says this even after God has given him a firsthand demonstration of the power that will be at his disposal as the chosen tool of God. What is going on here? Moses is not being protected by all of his Egyptian education. He is not being motivated by the wealth of his Egyptian cultural knowledge. He is not being heartened by his personal understanding of palace politics. None of these things are helping Moses at this point, because he is being betrayed by the fear of his own heart. And it is only in the face of God's anger that Moses finally goes.

Or think of the army of Israel in the valley of Elah, armed for battle but too afraid to fight. They stood there as the chosen army of the Most

High God, the Lord of Hosts, afraid to face the Philistine champion. It was an army suffering from a tragic case of identity amnesia. They forgot who they were. They forgot the promises they had been given. And because they did, they drew a false spiritual equation as they evaluated the moment. It wasn't these puny little soldiers against this huge giant; it was this puny giant against Almighty God. First Samuel 17 chronicles David's arriving. This shepherd, there to deliver provisions to his brothers, was a man of faith, a man who had experienced the rescuing power of God. So David couldn't understand why the army was not fighting. In an act of courage that is possible only for someone who knows who he is as the child of God and rests in what he has been given, David walks into that valley to face Goliath with nothing more than a shepherd's sling. David is drawing the right spiritual equation and knows that God will deliver the Philistine champion and his army into his hand. David knows that he fights not in the shadow of the glory of Goliath but in the brightness of the glory of God. It is the courage of the faith residing in his heart that propels him into that valley.

Or remember Elijah, who, after the great victory over the prophets of Baal on Mount Carmel, finds himself so alone, discouraged, and hopeless that he wishes he could die. First Kings 19 pictures for us this pathetic prophet who has completely lost his way and is convinced it's the end. He can see no way out. He is convinced that he is the only righteous man left, and from his vantage point it looks as though evil is going to win. God has to come to Elijah and return him to his senses. He is not alone; God's work is not done. Evil will not ultimately win. There are seven thousand faithful who are still left to carry on the work of God.

Think about what Paul says of his opposition of Peter, who was about to compromise a core principle of the gospel because he was afraid of what a certain group of people would think and how they would respond to him. He was about to act in a way that directly contradicted the message that he was called to represent, not because he lacked knowledge, experience, or skill but because, at the moment, his heart was ruled more by horizontal fear than vertical belief.

In each instance, with each leader, the thing that makes the difference at crucial-choice points is the condition of the person's heart. The heart is the inescapable X factor in ministry. Put two men with the exact same training, experience, and skill set next to one another, and it would be easy to conclude that they will respond in similar ways to the push and pull of local church ministry. It would be easy to conclude this, but dangerous. The potential for significant difference in the way these men function as pastors is as wide as the catalog of things that can rule a person's heart in ministry. It is naive to think that pastoral ministry is always propelled by love for Christ and his gospel. It is simplistic to conclude that people in ministry have a natural and abiding love for people. It is dangerous to conclude that everyone in ministry is working for the furtherance of the big kingdom. It is important to recognize that many people in ministry have been seduced by self-glory and have lost sight of the glory of God. Not all people in ministry do their work out of a humble sense of their own need. Ministries are derailed because leaders begin to think they have arrived and don't do the protective things that they warn everyone else to do. It's naive to think that pastors are free from sexual temptation, fear of man, envy, greed, pride, anger, doubt of God, bitterness, and idolatry. It is vital to remember that every pastor is in the middle of being reconstructed by God's grace.

So it is essential to know the heart of the man behind the knowledge, skill, experience, and ministry strategy before you call him to pastor God's flock. You can be assured that like God's leaders of old, he will face crucial personal- and ministry-choice points. In those significant moments, what will win the day and determine what he will do will be his heart because, like everyone else, it is inescapably true that whatever rules his heart will direct his life and his ministry. It is vital to get way, way beyond the profile that emerges from the data on his vitae.

CHAPTER FIVE

JOINTS AND LIGAMENTS

Pastor, have you ever asked yourself, who am I, and what do I spiritually need? Or have you ever thought about your pastor and asked, who is my pastor, and what does he need in order to remain spiritually healthy and grow in grace? Does it seem right and healthy that in many churches the functional reality is that no one gets less of the ministry of the body of Christ than the pastor does? Does it seem best that most pastors are allowed to live outside of or up above the body of Christ? If every pastor is, in fact, a man in the middle of his own sanctification, shouldn't he be receiving the normal range of the essential ministry of the body of Christ that God has ordained for every member of the church to receive? Is there any indication in the New Testament that the pastor is the exception to the normal rules that God has designed for the health and growth of his people? Is it possible that we have constructed a kind of relationship of the pastor to his congregation that cannot work? Could it be that we're asking something of our pastors that they will be unable to do? Is it biblical to tell pastors that they won't be able to be friends with anyone, that they must live in an isolation that we would say is unhealthy for anyone else?

THE BLIND LEADING THE BLIND

You only need to take seriously what the Bible has to say about the presence and power of remaining sin to know the great danger in allowing anyone to live separate from the essential ministry of the body of Christ, let alone the person who is charged with leading, guiding, and protecting that body as the representative of Christ. If Christ is the head of his body—and he is—then everything else is just body. The most influential pastor or ministry leader is a member of the body of Christ and therefore needs what the other members of the body need. There is no indication in the New Testament that the pastor is the exception to the rule of all that is said about the interconnectivity and necessary ministry of the body of Christ. What is true of the seemingly less significant members of the body is also true of the pastor. An intentional culture of pastoral separation and isolation is neither biblical nor spiritually healthy.

Let me suggest one passage, which I have written about before, that powerfully reinforces this point. It is Hebrews 3:12–13: "Take care, brothers, lest there be in any of you an evil, unbelieving heart, leading you to fall away from the living God. But exhort one another every day, as long as it is called 'today,' that none of you may be hardened by the deceitfulness of sin." This passage puts before us a critical warning and an essential call that together reinforce the presence and power of remaining sin and the need for the daily ministry of the body of Christ in the life of every member (pastor included) of the body of Christ.

Consider with me the *critical warning*. I don't know if you noticed it, but the warning in this passage is progressive. It pictures the progressive steps of the hardening of a believer's heart. (The greeting, "brothers," tells us this passage is written to believers.) The warning reads like this: "See to it that none of you has an evil—unbelieving, falling away—hardened heart." It is a picture of what sin does if undetected, unexposed, and unforsaken. Let me work through the steps with you.

It all begins with me giving way to sin in my life. I let things into my life that are outside the boundaries of what God has called me to be and do, things that God would name as "evil." Because I am a believer and the heart of stone has been taken out of me and replaced with a heart of flesh, my conscience bothers me when I sin. This is the beautiful, convicting ministry of the Holy Spirit. When my conscience is activated and bothered, I am faced with making one of two choices. The first and best choice is to admit that what I have done is wrong and place myself once again under the justifying mercies of Christ, receiving his forgiveness. Or I can erect some system of self-atonement that essentially argues for the rightness of what I've done. What I am doing here is making myself feel good about what God says is not good. I am participating in my own spiritual blindness. Every person still living with sin inside is a very skilled self-swindler. I think we do this way more often than we are aware.

So the pastor who has just become angry during an elders' meeting will tell himself he wasn't angry; he was just speaking like one of God's prophets: "Thus says the Lord!" The husband and wife who are gossiping about someone in their small group all the way home from the meeting will tell themselves that it isn't gossip; it's just a very extended and detailed prayer request. The tightfisted businessman who struggles to be giving will tell himself that he is just being a good steward of the resources that God has entrusted to him. We all have a perverse ability to make ourselves feel good about what is in no way good.

This is exactly what the next step in the hardening process is about. "Unbelieving" captures what we do to cover our sin and defend our righteousness. Rather than a simple faith and rest in the accurate diagnosis of the Word of God and the sufficient grace of Christ, we work to tell ourselves that we are not really, in this particular instance, sinners in need of forgiving mercy, because what we have done is not, in fact, wrong. Our self-atoning arguments are acts of pride, rebellion, and unbelief.

This street-level pride, rebellion, and unbelief invariably give sin further room to operate. Because we have not confessed, repented, and sought the forgiving, transforming, empowering, and delivering grace that we need, we have opened ourselves up to more of sin's ugly work. The third part in this sad progression, "falling away," captures this well. It is a firm acceptance of the diagnostic of Scripture and a firm rest in the grace of Christ that anchor us against the storms of temptation, and when we cut that anchor rope, we will always end up drifting further.

Where we finally end is with a "hardened" heart. What once bothered us doesn't bother us anymore. What once activated our conscience doesn't seem to anymore. What we knew was outside of God's boundaries, and therefore was functionally outside of ours, lives inside our boundaries, and it doesn't matter to us anymore. It is a scary place to be. The hard heart is a stony heart. It's not malleable anymore. It's hard and resistant to change, no longer tender and responsive to the squeeze of the hands of the Spirit. There is evil in our hearts and in the acts of our hands, and we're okay with it. Could there be a more dangerous place for a believer to be?

Let me be candid here. I've been in this place as a pastor. I held a bitter list of wrongs against people in my congregation, and I worked to be okay with it. I gossiped about people I was called to care for, and it didn't bother me. I was envious of the ministry of others, and it did not grieve me. At times I preached to gain the respect of someone in my congregation and did not see that as the idolatry it was. And because I didn't see these things as the evil that they were, I felt no need for change.

Now, the question that every reader should be asking at this point is how can these scary steps of hardening take place in the life of a believer? It is here where you need the writer of Hebrews' theology of remaining sin. Essentially he says that this is able to happen because sin is fundamentally deceptive. You will never understand the warning of this passage and the call that follows until you understand the theology of spiritual blindness that is the epicenter of both the warning and the call.

Sin is deceptive, and think with me about who it deceives first. I have no difficulty recognizing the sin of the people around me, but I can be quite unprepared when my sin is pointed out. Sin deceives ten out of ten people reading this book. But it is not enough even to say that; there is more that needs to be said. It needs to be noted that spiritual blindness is not like physical blindness. When you are physically blind, you know that you are blind, and you do things to compensate for this significant physical deficit. But spiritually blind people are not only blind; they are blind to their own blindness. They are blind, but they think that they see well. So the spiritually blind person walks around with the delusion that no one has a more accurate view of him than he does. He thinks he sees and is unaware of the powerfully important things in his heart that he absolutely does not see at all.

This is where the *essential call* of the passage comes in. The call is to encourage (or exhort) each other daily. Here's the significant explanation as to why this call is essential: "that none of you be hardened by the deceitfulness of sin." The blinding ability of sin is so powerful and persuasive that you and I literally need daily intervention. What the writer of Hebrews is crushing with this warning and call is any allegiance we might have to an isolated, individualized, "Jesus and me" Christianity. He is arguing for the essentiality of the ministry of others in the life of every believer. Obviously, this includes the pastor. None of us is wired to live this Christian life alone. None of us is safe living separated and unknown. Each of us, whether pastor or congregant, needs the eyes of others in order to see ourselves with clarity and accuracy. And what is this daily ministry of intervention protecting us from? The answer should sober every one of us: the grace of having our private conversations interrupted by the insight-giving ministry of others is protecting us from becoming spiritually blinded to the point of the hardening of our hearts. The author argues here that personal spiritual insight is the product of community. It's very difficult to get it by yourself. Perhaps every pastor needs to humbly recognize that because of the blinding power of remaining sin, self-examination is a community project. Every pastor needs people in his life in order to see himself with biblical accuracy.

This means that pastors who convince themselves that they are able to live outside of God's regular system of help and protection are in danger of becoming increasingly blind and hard of heart. This means that in their blindness they begin to think of themselves as more righteous than they actually are, and because they think they are more righteous than they actually are, they are resistant to change.

This means they will not hunger for the exhortation and admonition of others. They will not respond well when being reminded of their ongoing need for change. They will not work well with others because they will tend to think that they are right and know best. Thinking that they are right and know best means that they will not listen well and work as well as someone who is convinced that his walk with God is a community project.

It also means that they will struggle to be patient with people who are messing up or have lost their way. Self-righteous people tend not to be patient and understanding in the face of the failure of others. This goes back to the reality that no one gives grace better than a person who knows he desperately needs it himself. This self-righteous blindness also means that they will not deal very well with opposition and accusation. They will not see these things as tools of uncomfortable grace sent by a God who is continuing his work in them. Because they are content with who they are, they will wonder why God has singled them out for this particular difficulty, in moments giving way to questioning the goodness and wisdom of God.

I have talked with many pastors whose real struggle isn't first with the hardship of ministry, the lack of appreciation and involvement of people, or difficulties with fellow leaders. No, the real struggle they are having, one that is very hard for a pastor to admit, is with God. What has caused ministry to become hard and burdensome is disappointment with and anger at God. It's hard to represent someone you have come to doubt. It's hard to encourage others to functionally trust someone you're not sure you trust. It is nearly impossible in ministry to give away what you yourself do not have.

Could this passage be a more needed and accurate diagnosis, warning, and call to every pastor, no matter how long he's been in ministry, no matter where he is located, and no matter the size of the church he serves?

LIVING IN THE DANGER ZONE

Joe and Judy entered ministry with a mutual sense of excitement and calling. They could not believe that they were called to the privilege of doing ministry for a living. They loved the church they had attended for years, the place where their gifts and calling had been recognized. They loved being interns and then members of the staff and finally the honor of being chosen as the leaders of the newest church plant. It all seemed like a dream come true. They had lived in vibrant, mutually ministering community. People had spoken into their lives almost daily. They simply were never left to their own view of themselves. They were never expected to make it on their own. It was expected that they would mess up at points or lose their way. Protecting and preventing love was all around—love that was candid, encouraging, confronting, forgiving, and hopeful. Because they had grown so used to it, Joe and Judy left to plant the new church, seriously underestimating the importance of the ministry of personal insight and growth that they were leaving behind. They had no idea that they were stepping into the danger zone where no Christian, let alone a pastor, should attempt to live.

Almost immediately things began to change inside Joe, changes that he neither saw nor was concerned about. As a young pastor with a committed core group and a zeal to bring the gospel to his community, Joe began to deal with heart issues that he hadn't dealt with before, although he didn't recognize the significance of these issues. And he surely had no idea that these concerns would lead him into the danger zone and almost become the undoing of his ministry. I first met with Joe and his wife when they were just on the cusp of throwing in the towel. Judy said it this way: "All I long for is the freedom to live with a man who is not in ministry. I can't stand what it has done to Joe and our family. I'm done. I just can't do this anymore, and I think Joe is in no condition to lead others."

How did Joe and Judy get to this disheartening and discouraging place? The journey from ministry excitement to personal danger and ministry discouragement began with changes in Joe's heart. Perhaps these changes won't seem very significant or dangerous to you, but they almost led to this gifted man's undoing. Almost the minute they arrived to plant the church, Joe began to feel burdens that he hadn't felt before. He shared these burdens with no one, not even Judy. As the leader of this core group of courageous people, who had left a vibrant church to give themselves to this new ministry, Joe felt a huge pressure not to do anything that would disappoint. He felt more pressure than he had ever felt before to be sure to always say and do the right thing. He did not want people to be concerned at those moments when he felt weak, overwhelmed, unable, or afraid. And he surely didn't want Judy to see those things, because, of all people, she had been willing to leave much and risk much to follow him to this new place of ministry. He felt the need to act encouraged, hopeful, and assured (the operative term here is *act*), even when he wasn't. And in doing this, he began to be comfortable with a disharmony between his public ministry persona and the actual realities of his heart and life.

He told himself that this was important because he didn't want people to begin to question their involvement as a result of questioning his ability to lead. In ways of which he was not aware, Joe began to wall himself off from people. He got good at giving generalized nonanswers to personal questions. He got good at dispensing biblical, theological platitudes instead of talking about what he was really thinking and feeling. Yes, a pastor needs to be wise in what he discloses to whom, but he must not wall himself completely off from the body of Christ and name that as the cost of the ministry to which he has been called. But that is exactly what Joe did and what many, many pastors are doing around the world. Not only are they living in isolation, but also they are convinced that it is what they have been called to do. They name their isolation not as a danger but as a good and mature choice. Many young pastors tell me that they have been counseled by the more senior pastors, who are mentoring them, to live in isolation.

Joe worried about how the knowledge of his struggles would harm people's hope in the power of the gospel. He didn't want people to question the gospel because it didn't look as though the gospel was working in the life of their pastor. He wondered how they could trust God's help if it didn't look as if God was helping their pastor. So without there being one conscious moment of decision, Joe went into hiding. It seemed natural to him, the cost of his calling. Sure, he would say theological things about his need for grace, but never in a way that would lead others to seriously think that their pastor was a spiritually needy man.

Yet being the man that he thought he needed to be, working to be more publicly righteous than he actually was, was exhausting and burdensome. Even in more informal gatherings, Joe didn't relax. So he didn't enjoy these gatherings and would look for reasons not to participate. He had looked forward to the freedom and joy of being able to use and express his gifts as a senior pastor, but he didn't feel free, and he wasn't experiencing the joy that he thought he would experience. Joe was convinced of something that I have had many pastors say to me as well: he was convinced that everyone else in the body of Christ could confess sin, but he could not and must not.

Not only did Joe's isolation significantly add to the burden of pastoral ministry, but it also did something that was even more dangerous. It left Joe to his own blindness. It left him to his rationalizations, excuses, defenses, and self-atoning arguments. I'm not being hard on Joe here. These things are the tendencies of every sinner, because one of the most powerful components of spiritual blindness is self-deception. There is no one we swindle more than we swindle ourselves. There is no one we run to defend more than we do ourselves. And like every other spiritually blind person, Joe was blind to his blindness. In fact, Joe's blindness was even harder for him to acknowledge because his ministry gifts, skill, and discipline made it look to him that he was doing okay. But he wasn't okay.

Increasingly Joe was allowing himself to be okay with things that he should not be okay with: a hurtful poke at another person, gossip about a fellow leader, impatience in the middle of a meeting, walking away angry from a conversation, harboring bitterness against certain people in the church, infrequency in his time of personal worship and devotion, and growing impatience, irritation, and isolation at home. Judy began to notice what she would now characterize as a changed

Joe, but the changes didn't happen in an instant. It was a process of Joe's doing and saying things that he once wouldn't have done; but what concerned Judy was that this no longer seemed to bother Joe. When Joe had given in to these temptations in the past, his pattern had always been to confess and make right what needed to be made right.

Not only was Judy concerned that Joe wasn't confessing, but he would also get angry quickly when Judy would try to point out the problems. He would tell her that so much of his ministry was about being scrutinized and criticized by people that he didn't need to come home and have it happen there as well. Judy also noticed Joe separating himself from the family. He spent way too much time Facebooking the world and a scary amount of time numbing himself with television. And there seemed to be no way Judy could talk to him about it, and if the kids disturbed him, Joe responded with anything but parental patience and grace.

The separation between Joe's public ministry persona and his private life became too much for Judy to bear. She began to feel that ministry was destroying Joe and her family. Quietly she began to hope and pray that Joe would come to the end of himself and want to get out of ministry. Joe was in pastoral isolation and survival mode. He was cranking out his duties, but the joy was gone. When Judy looked at Joe and watched him struggle through another week, it really did look as if Jesus had left the building. She could take it no more. She loved Joe too much. She thought his calling was too holy. So, she gave that fateful ultimatum to Joe: "It's me or the ministry."

I wish I could say that Joe's story is unique, but it is not. The details are individual, but I have heard the contours of this story again and again. The problem is bigger than the sin of an individual pastor. There are changes needed in the shape of pastoral culture. How can we realistically expect anyone in the middle of the sanctification process to live outside of one of God's most important means of personal insight and growth and be spiritually healthy at the same time? How can we ask pastors to confess what they, because of their isolation, don't see? How can we ask them to confess when they are convinced that honest confession would cost them not only respect but also their jobs? And how can we expect them to repent and turn from what they have not confessed? How is it that in many situations we have come to expect that the one leading the body of Christ can do well spiritually while getting less of the ministry of the body of Christ than everyone he has been called to lead? Why would we be surprised that pastors struggle with sin? Why would we think that pastors do not need to be lovingly confronted and rebuked? Why would it surprise us to know that pastors too fall into identity amnesia and begin to seek horizontally what they have already been given in Christ? Why would we conclude that pastors are protected from self-righteousness and defensiveness just because they are in full-time ministry? Why would we assume that pastors who have not been educated in the ways of grace would rest in the righteousness of Christ and not defend and parade their own?

Is it safe to assume that your pastor is loving his wife, children, and extended family well? Is it safe to assume that he is using his time and money well? Is it safe to assume that he is honoring God with what he does in his most private moments? Is it safe to assume that he is as committed to the opportunities and responsibilities of his calling as he should be? Is it safe to assume that he works to make sure that there is living agreement between his public proclamations and his private life? Doesn't every member of the body of Christ need the ministry of the body of Christ, including the pastor?

A BETTER, MORE HEALTHY WAY

Let me suggest several steps that can work to bring pastors out of isolation and into more regular contact with the essential and normal ministries of the body of Christ. These are written to pastors and those who care for them.

1) REQUIRE YOUR PASTOR TO ATTEND A SMALL GROUP HE DOESN'T LEAD.

It is a simple but very effective way for a small group of people to get to know their pastor, to see him in a more normal setting, and to learn the places where he needs ministry and prayer. The pastors I have talked to who are doing this have all reported how spiritually beneficial it has been.

2) PASTOR, SEEK OUT A SPIRITUALLY MATURE PERSON TO MENTOR YOU AT ALL TIMES.

Pastor, make sure you are being pastored the entire time you are pastoring others. Seek out a mature and reliable person with whom you can share your heart. Work to build with that person a sturdy bond of trust. Refuse to live without this kind of person in your life. Meet with this individual as frequently as possible. Share your struggles with him and be humble enough to listen when pastorally spoken to.

3) ESTABLISH A PASTORS' WIVES' SMALL GROUP.

At Tenth Presbyterian Church, where I served for the last several years, there is a beautiful monthly gathering of all the pastors' wives. It is a "what is said here stays here" gathering. The main part of this gathering is extended sharing by each of the pastors' wives, followed by an extensive time of prayer for each. Not only has this been an amazing help and protection for each of the wives, but also it has stimulated and directed each to minister to her husband more boldly and more wisely. This may be the most effective small group in the church. If your church is small and does not have multiple pastors, try to establish something similar between several churches.

4) PASTOR, BE COMMITTED TO APPROPRIATE SELF-DISCLOSURE IN YOUR PREACHING.

There are surely struggles that you should not share in a public ministry setting, but there are many that you can. Not only do these often become the most effective illustrations of the importance and practicality of the truths you exegete, but also they remind people that, like them, you too need rescuing, forgiving, empowering grace. When you do this, people quit looking at you and saying, "If only I could be like my pastor." No, they look through you and see the glory of an ever-present Christ. You quit being a painting that they gaze at, and you start being a window to the One who is your and their hope. It has impressed me, when I share personally in preaching, how many people let me know later that they have prayed for me.

5) BE SURE THAT YOUR PASTOR AND HIS FAMILY ARE REGULARLY INVITED INTO THE HOMES OF FAMILIES IN YOUR CHURCH.

Determine that you will not let your pastor and his family live in isolation. Encourage the people in your church to invite him and his family over for a summer barbeque or a swim in the backyard pool. Invite them over to watch a game during the playoffs or to enjoy the meal that has been passed down in the family for generations. Take the pastor and his wife out to eat. Invite him to go golfing or fishing with the group of guys who do that regularly. Get them out of hiding and invite them into situations where they can relax and just be as ordinary as possible.

6) MAKE SURE THERE IS SOMEONE WHO IS REGULARLY MENTORING YOUR PASTOR'S WIFE.

Every pastor's wife needs a "go to" person that she can call spontaneously in a moment of need and be sure that a listening ear and help will be on the other end. Such an individual can be trusted with the delicate things that the pastor's wife may need to discuss and will need to be willing to be available, as much as anyone could, 24/7.

7) MAKE SURE YOUR PASTOR AND HIS WIFE HAVE THE MEANS TO BE REGULARLY OUT OF THE HOUSE AND AWAY FOR WEEKENDS WITH ONE ANOTHER.

Make sure that the busyness of family and the endless demands of ministry don't combine to cause the pastor and his wife to fail to give their marriage the attention and maintenance it needs. Do everything you can to give your pastor and his wife the help, time, and resources they need to get out of the house on a regular basis and away for the weekend as frequently as is feasible. Don't allow your pastor and his wife to assume that tensions between family and ministry are acceptable and unavoidable. Help your pastor and his wife to have all the resources possible to give their relationship the focus and investment that it needs, to be a place of unity, understanding, and love.

8) MAKE SURE COUNSELING HELP IS ALWAYS AVAILABLE TO THE PASTOR, HIS WIFE, AND THEIR FAMILY.

Assure your pastor from day one that there is counseling help available whenever it is needed. Pastors, be honest about the condition of your heart and seek help quickly and willingly when needed. Pastor, are you telling yourself that it is okay, the duty of your calling, to live in isolation? Who knows you well enough to speak truth to you when you need it? Who works to protect you from you? How accurate is the view of the body of Christ as to who you really are? Is the culture of your church such that you can be comfortable there confessing your sin? Are you fearful of any self-disclosure in public ministry settings? Does your wife live with the pain of the differences between the public and private man?

▲ ▲ ▲

May fewer and fewer of those who are called to lead us live in isolation and separation from the body of Christ, and may that lead to more and more pastors who are tender and humble examples, in both their private and public lives, of both the need for and the transforming power of the grace of the Lord Jesus Christ.

CHAPTER SIX

THE MISSING COMMUNITY

I was raised in the "Jesus and me" privatized, individualized Christianity of the fundamentalism of the '60s and '70s. The closest our church got to an actual functioning, ministry-oriented body of Christ was a rare pastoral visit and the Wednesday night prayer meeting. No one knew my father and mother—I mean, really knew them. No one had a clue what was going on in our home. No one helped my father to see through the blindness that allowed him to live a double life of skilled deception and duplicity. No one knew how troubled my mother was beneath her encyclopedic knowledge of Scripture. No one knew. We were a Christian family in active participation in a vibrant church, but what we were involved in lacked one of the primary and essential ingredients of healthy New Testament Christianity: a trained, mobilized, and functioning body of Christ. It was Christianity devoid of Ephesians 4, 1 Corinthians 12, and Hebrews 3:12–13.

For much of my Christian life and a portion of my ministry, I had no idea that my walk with God was a community project. I had no idea that the Christianity of the New Testament is distinctly relational, from beginning to end. I understood none of the dangers inherent in attempting to live the Christian life on my own. I had no awareness of the blinding power of remaining sin, which was discussed in the last chapter. I had no idea that I was living outside of God's normal means of sightedness, encouragement, conviction, strength, and growth. I had no idea how much consumerism and how little true participation marked the body of Christ. I had no idea of the importance of the private ministry of the Word to the health of the believer. I had no idea.

I have now come to understand that I need others in my life. I now know that I need to commit myself to living in *intentionally intrusive, Christ-centered, grace-driven, redemptive community.* I now know it's my job to seek this community out, to invite people to interrupt my private conversation, and to say things to me that I couldn't or wouldn't say to myself. I have realized how much I need warning, encouragement, rebuke, correction, protection, grace, and love. I now see myself as connected to others, not because I have made the choice but because of the wise design of the one who is the head of the body, the Lord Jesus Christ. I cannot allow myself to think that I am smarter than him. I cannot allow myself to think that I am stronger than I am. I cannot assign to myself a level of maturity that I do not have. I cannot begin to believe that I am able to live outside of God's normal means of spiritual growth and be okay. I cannot allow the level of my spiritual health to be defined by my ministry experience and success or by my theological knowledge. I cannot let myself be lulled to sleep by the congratulatory comments on ministry weekends by people who mean well but really don't know me. I cannot let myself think that my marriage can be healthy if I live in functional isolation from the body of Christ.

Since, as one who has remaining sin still inside of him, it is right to say that the greatest danger in my life exists inside of me and not outside of me, then wouldn't it also be the height of naivety or arrogance to think that I would be okay left to myself? No, not for a moment would I forget or diminish the convicting ministry of the indwelling Holy Spirit, but I would posit that the Spirit uses instruments (his transforming Word brought faithfully by his people and empowered by his ever-present grace).

Having said all of this, it is my grief to say that individualized, privatized Christianity still lives. Sadly, it lives in the lives and ministries of many pastors who have forged or been allowed to forge a life that is lived above or outside of the body of Christ. It happens this way for many pastors. Their spiritual life became immediately more privatized when they left their home church to go to seminary in another city. For many, the seminary became their primary spiritual community, a community that was neither personal nor pastoral in the way it handled Scripture and related to the student. Having graduated from an environment where, for three or more years, they were not pastored and had a rather casual relationship to a local church, they are now called by a church that doesn't really know them. This is all magnified by the fact that they are not joining the church per se; no, they have been called to lead it. So they are not entering into a situation of naturally expected peer, mutual-ministry relationships. They are not afforded the normal expectations and protections that anyone else is offered when they join the church. It is a potentially unbiblical and unhealthy culture that does not protect the pastor and does not guard his ministry from danger.

Pastor, you know that every day you give personal empirical evidence that you have not yet arrived. Every day you think, desire, say, and do things that point to the existence of remaining sin within your heart. Since this is true of each of us, is it not also true that we need to live in a willingly submissive commitment to God's normal means of protecting and growing his still-being-sanctified children?

A THEOLOGY OF ESSENTIALITY

I want to consider with you three very familiar passages of Scripture that need a second look, particularly for how they speak into normal pastoral culture. Before we look at these three passages, I want to first give you the helicopter view of the ministry of the Word in the life of the local church. The Bible envisions two essential, interdependent, and complementary ministries of the Word. First there is the public ministry of the Word. This is the regularly scheduled public teaching and preaching of God's Word to gathered groups in the church. This ministry makes up the *formative discipline* of the church. Every member is discipled from the pulpit with the same body of foundational perspective-altering, life-shaping truths. Here all of God's people are placed on the same tracks and headed in the same direction. Because this public ministry of the Word is done with groups of people, it must be general in its consideration of audience and therefore in its application. God gifts and sets apart certain people for this important formative ministry.

Because it is also important that God's Word be applied with concrete specificity to the lives of individual believers so that they are clear as to what it looks like to follow Christ in the context of their particular situation and relationships, God has ordained a second, complementary ministry of the Word, its private ministry. This makes up the *corrective discipline* of the church. This ministry does not have a different body of content. No, it takes the general truths that everyone has been hearing and applies them with specificity to the lives of individual believers so that they can more concretely understand what it means to live in light of the things they are being taught. The radical Word culture of the church as God designed it drafts all of God's children to be willing, envisioned, trained, and mobilized participants in this second ministry of the Word. Private ministry of the Word depends on public ministry of the Word to give people their formative foundation, and the public ministry looks to private ministry to counsel people into understanding the specific practical life implications of what they have been learning as the Word has been taught publicly. Neither ministry is a luxury. Each is an essential part of God's bi-factoral, Word-centered growth strategy for the local church.

Now let's apply this model to the life and ministry of the pastor. The first passage is Ephesians 4:11–16:

> And he gave the apostles, the prophets, the evangelists, the shepherds and teachers, to equip the saints for the work of ministry, for building up the body of Christ, until we all attain to the unity of the faith and of the knowledge of the Son of God, to mature manhood, to the measure of the stature of the fullness of Christ, so that we may no longer be children, tossed to and fro by the waves and carried about by every wind of doctrine, by human cunning, by craftiness in deceitful schemes. Rather, speaking the truth in love, we are to grow up in every way into him who is the head, into Christ, from whom the whole body, joined and held together by every joint with which it is equipped, when each part is working properly, makes the body grow so that it builds itself up in love.

As I work through these passages, you pastors who are reading through with me are going to have to resist the spiritual pride that causes you to hit the shutoff switch in the middle of the discussions because in your heart of hearts you really don't think all of this applies to you. Ephesians 4 has a very clear "already–not yet" structure. Already each of us has been gifted with redeeming grace. Each of us has been indwelt by the Holy Spirit. Each of us has been blessed with a now-illumined Bible. But not yet do we fully and perfectly understand our faith. Not yet have we been fully matured into the likeness of Christ. Not yet is the deceptive war for our hearts over. We live and minister smack-dab in the middle, and in the middle God has set up essential tools for our protection and growth. None of us will be safe or healthy if we tell ourselves that we can live outside of these essential tools.

What are the goals of the "everybody-all-the-time" ministry that Paul lays out in this passage? The goals are unity of the faith, knowledge of the Son of God, and maturity in every way in Christ. The goals encourage us to humbly admit that all of us—yes, even pastors—live on the short side of these goals. None of us exists in fully unified communities of faith, none of us knows Christ as fully as he can be known, and none of us is fully grown into the likeness of Jesus. So what is the implication of that humble admission? It is that each of us—yes, even pastors—needs to joyfully submit to God's means of bringing these goals into completion in our hearts and lives.

What are the dangers inherent in convincing ourselves that we can live outside of God's normal means of personal spiritual health and growth? They are equally clear in this passage. If we attempt to do what we are not wired by redemption to do, we will be susceptible to lingering immaturity in specific areas of our life and to doctrinal error or confusion, and we will live in danger of being deceived. Think with me for a moment. Each of us is able to cite occurrences of each danger in our own circles of pastors. I have counseled pastors who damaged their churches because they had failed to grow up. I have experienced churches damaged by pastors who were moved away by the latest wind of fad doctrine. I was a self-deceived pastor, thinking I knew myself better than I did and thinking I was more spiritually well off than I actually was. These warnings are not just for the average Christian but for every member of the body of Christ. They call everyone in ministry to humbly admit that in the middle of the already–not yet, there is a war that is still taking place for the rulership of our hearts. And because there is, we all need the warning, protective, encouraging, rebuking, growth-producing ministry of the body of Christ.

Now, what methodology has God chosen to employ to guard, grow, and protect us? It is the public and private ministry of the Word. This passage particularly emphasizes the essentiality of private, body-member-to-body-member ministry. Again the words are specific and clear: "Speaking the truth in love . . . joined and held together by every joint . . . when each part is working properly . . . builds itself up in love." There is no indication in this passage that any member of Christ's body is able or permitted to live outside of the essential ministry of the body of Christ. But I think it is exactly at this point that we can be tempted to draw conclusions from this passage that it doesn't actually teach. Because it ascribes to the pastor the responsibility of training God's people for their member-to-member ministry function, I am afraid that we have unwittingly concluded that the pastor is above a need of what the rest of the body needs and does. But the passage never teaches this; it actually teaches the opposite. The pastor is in the unique position of not only training the body for this ministry but also of personally needing the very ministry for which he trains them. Remember, the words here—"every joint," "each part"—do not leave much room for exemptions. Again, I think of it this way: if Christ is the head of his body, then everything else is just body, including the pastor, and therefore the pastor needs what the body has been designed to deliver.

First Corinthians 12:14–25 in ways presents this even more forcefully:

> For the body does not consist of one member but of many. If the foot should say, "Because I am not a hand, I do not belong to the

> body," that would not make it any less a part of the body. And if the ear should say, "Because I am not an eye, I do not belong to the body," that would not make it any less a part of the body. If the whole body were an eye, where would be the sense of hearing? If the whole body were an ear, where would be the sense of smell? But as it is, God arranged the members in the body, each one of them, as he chose. If all were a single member, where would the body be? As it is, there are many parts, yet one body. The eye cannot say to the hand, "I have no need of you," nor again the head to the feet, "I have no need of you." On the contrary, the parts of the body that seem to be weaker are indispensable, and on those parts of the body that we think less honorable we bestow the greater honor, and our unpresentable parts are treated with greater modesty, which our more presentable parts do not require. But God has so composed the body, giving greater honor to the part that lacked it, that there may be no division in the body, but that the members may have the same care for one another.

The picture here is the body of Christ as a functioning organism of many mutually essential, interrelating, mutually contributing members. The interconnectedness and the interdependency of these members are so essential to the proper health, function, and growth of the body that Paul says it is impossible for one member to say to another, "I simply don't need you," or "I am able to function quite well on my own, thank you," or "I have grown to the point where I no longer need what you have to offer." In the context of Paul's word picture of a healthy physical body, these assertions would take a denial of inescapable realities. So it is with the body of Christ. So it is, I would add, with the spiritual healthiness and ministry vitality of the pastor. He is a member of the body of Christ who himself desperately needs the ministry of the very body he has been called to train and lead. The model is of a man in need of help in training people to be ready to give him the very same help. You simply cannot escape what these passages are teaching.

Darrel stood before me during a break at a major conference and wept. He couldn't have cared less who was looking at him or what they heard him say. He was just that desperate. He had the appearance of a completely beaten, totally broken man, but he was a God-gifted, divinely appointed pastor. No, he wasn't in a proud war with his leaders, he hadn't committed adultery, and he was not addicted to pornography or substances. He was an angry, discouraged, embittered, and now desperate man. Through his tears he said, "Paul, I just don't know how to go home. No one knows me there. No one knows what is going on in my family. No one knows what is in my heart. No one knows that I force myself to crank out sermons every week. No one knows that I hate most of the meetings that I lead. No one knows that my wife and I bicker and fight our way through week after week. No one knows that my children are beginning to hate the gospel because of me. No one knows that I numb myself with hours of television. I have no one to talk to, not one close relationship in the entire church. My family lives in isolation, but I don't think anyone notices. My wife has some friends, but she's very careful about what she says. If I just stopped a meeting and began to confess what is really going on with me, I don't think my leaders could deal with it. Paul, if I come clean, if I let people in, I'm done. I don't know how to go home and face this stuff."

Does Darrel's situation sound extreme to you? It doesn't to me, because I've heard his cry again and again. No, it hasn't always reached this level of desperation, but there are way too many pastors out there who have lost their joy, who are cranking it out. There are way too many bitter and angry people in ministry who are carrying around a self-protective list of previously experienced wrongs. There are way too many pastors living in isolation who are in trouble, and they don't know it. There are way too many congregations and leadership boards that have a distorted, unrealistic, idealized image of their pastor. There are way too many ministry families that are unprotected because they are not being properly pastored. There are way too many pastors in survival mode. There are way too many pastors' wives who fantasize about what it would be like to be out of the ministry. There are way too many children who bear the daily brunt of the ministry father's bitterness and anger. There simply is way too much functional anonymity in the pulpits of our churches.

The third of our passages specifically defines the nature of the essential private ministry of the Word that is the calling of the body of Christ. In this way Colossians 3:15–17 is very helpful:

> And let the peace of Christ rule in your hearts, to which indeed you were called in one body. And be thankful. Let the word of Christ dwell in you richly, teaching and admonishing one another in all wisdom, singing psalms and hymns and spiritual songs, with thankfulness in your hearts to God. And whatever you do, in word or deed, do everything in the name of the Lord Jesus, giving thanks to God the Father through him.

Paul envisions a well-prepared body of Christ with the Word of God dwelling in their hearts, now ready to do what God has designed the body of Christ to do. And what is that? Again, Paul is very specific: *teach* and *admonish*. Now, let's be honest. In most contexts, what Paul is describing would be quite radical, maybe even unsettling. He is actually proposing that every believer is designed to have a teaching function in the life of every believer. It really is an "all-of-God's-people-all-of-the-time" paradigm. This means that it's unhealthy for any church and its pastor if, in that church, the pastor is the only teacher. It is assumed here that every teacher, no matter where God has placed him or her in the body, needs to be taught, and all the people being taught need also to teach.

Now, notice again the two descriptive words that Paul uses: *teach* and *admonish*. To put the most basic definitions on these terms is to say that *teaching* enables you to see life God's way. It is embedding the story of life in the larger story of redemption. *Admonishing* is helping you to see yourself God's way. It is standing you before the perfect mirror of God's Word so that you are confronted with the reality of who you really are. There is not a day when every member of the body of Christ does not need to be taught, helped to identify those remaining artifacts of an ungospelized worldview. There is also not a day when we don't need to be admonished, confronted with the fact that we still look into the world's carnival mirrors and carry around distorted opinions of who we are.

Pastor, you too need to be surrounded by well-trained teachers and faithful, loving admonishers. And you are in danger if anonymity allows you to be the only regular teacher you hear and to live void of a protective circle of grace-motivated admonishers.

THE CYCLE OF DANGER

1) UNHELPFUL ASSUMPTIONS

In many cases the cycle of isolation and danger begins when the church that calls the pastor makes incorrect and unhelpful assumptions about the person they have called. Sadly, in many cases the person being called has not lived in protective and productive redemptive community for years. Having separated from the nurture of his home church, where his gifts were recognized, he goes off to a place where the faith has been academized and compartmentalized, being taught by professors who do not presume to function as the pastors of their students. In many cases, because he is working as well as engaging in the rigors of theological education, he has little remaining time to have but a cursory relationship to a local church. This probably also means he's been a bit of a distracted husband and absentee dad. Meanwhile his own relationship to Scripture has been more about completing assignments than a devotional nurturing of his soul.

But the church that has called him tends to assume that because his gifts and some level of maturity have been recognized and because he is now a biblical scholar, trained for the pastorate, he is spiritually healthy and able to live without the normal protections and encouragements that they would want for any other believer. So a culture of untoward assumptions and functional pastoral isolation is often set up from the moment of the first interview.

2) UNREALISTIC EXPECTATIONS

It should be obvious that the unhelpful assumptions made as the pastor is coming to lead the church would be fruit in a whole set of unrealistic expectations. The biggest is that many churches simply don't expect their pastor to struggle with sin. But he is not sin-free! Since he is still being sanctified, sin still remains and is being progressively eradicated. They don't expect him to get discouraged in the middle of the war for the gospel. They don't expect him to be tempted toward bitterness or envy. They expect him to be a model husband and father. They don't expect him to be lazy or to settle for mediocrity. They don't expect that in moments of self-protection he will be tempted to be antisocial and controlling. They expect that he will be able to joyfully carry an unrealistic job description that would overwhelm anyone this side of Jesus's return. They expect that he will be content with significantly less pay than most people with his level of education. They expect that his wife is so fully committed to ministry herself that his coming to the church is actually a two-for-one deal. They don't expect that there will be moments when he is tempted to doubt the goodness of God. They don't expect that in a meeting or in the pulpit, fear of man will keep him from doing or saying the things that God calls him to do and say. They don't expect to hire a flawed man who is still desperately in need of the very grace that he is called to offer and exegete for others.

3) RETICENCE TO SPEAK WITH CANDOR

In most situations the local-church pastoral culture (the nature and character of the relationship of a pastor to his leaders and congregation) is set in the early days of his ministry in that particular church. If the leaders that called him have sought to know the man behind the gifts, experience, and skills, and if they have alerted him to the fact that he is entering an intentionally intrusive, Christ-centered, grace-driven redemptive community, then what follows will be requirements that he participate in and be a recipient of the ministry of the body of Christ and the promise of those who seek to build relationship with him as instruments of seeing in his life. If the calling process has failed to go after the heart of the potential pastor, and if in the early days it hasn't been clear that the church fully intends to pastor their pastor—not just to hold him accountable but to minister the gospel of

Jesus Christ to his soul—then he will probably conduct most of his ministry in the context of personal isolation coupled with a large network of terminally casual relationships. Both the body and the leaders will be reticent to speak to him with biblical candor tempered with love, and he will be reticent to make confession to people who aren't used to having that kind of relationship with their pastor. There will probably be more talking about him than talking to him, and he will probably do more hiding than confessing. It simply is far from what God designed this community of grace, called "the church," to be and to do.

4) ABSENCE OF TIMELY INTERVENTION

The "exhort one another daily" command of Hebrews 3:13 tells us that because of remaining sin, our capacity for self-deception is so great that we need regular, even daily intervention. We all need this ministry of intervention, where someone interrupts our private conversation and helps us to see ourselves with greater biblical accuracy, until sin is no more. But when a local church makes wrong assumptions about their pastor, does not invite him into a culture of loving candor, and allows him to live in functional separation from the body of Christ, he will not be the recipient of the kind of Christ-centered, heart-rescuing intervention that every pastor needs.

5) LOSS OF RESPECT IN THE FACE OF PERSONAL REVELATIONS

What then happens is that the pastor will tend to live in a continual state of spiritual hiding with a growing separation between his private and public life and will make confession to his fellow leaders and perhaps to the wider body only when struggles have progressed to a point where they cannot be hidden any more. No, it's not as if he is participating in a huge spiritual cover-up; it is simply that this is the way a culture of assumptions, silence, and separation operates. When he finally makes confession, he comes crashing down from the unrealistic and unbiblical pedestal that he has been standing on. The community surrounding him is shocked and dismayed and suffers a huge loss of respect for him and is therefore unable to minister the grace of the gospel to him in the way that he has done and so desperately needs himself.

6) DYSFUNCTIONAL SYSTEMS OF RESTORATION

In the face of this shock and loss of respect, the local church is tempted to just want to move beyond the ministry of this man and replace him with someone they can once again respect and follow. So the church gets rid of its problem and moves beyond its leadership crisis, but the pastor and his family are the casualty. The heart issues of the man have not been dealt with biblically, he has no greater personal spiritual insight, he has not received the transforming grace of the gospel, the leaders he leaves behind are tempted to be a little more cynical, the weaknesses in their leadership culture are unaddressed, and he is tempted to take on the bitterness of a victim. Is this too dark of a picture? I wish I could say it is, but I have personally witnessed this sad progression.

7) LACK OF DISCERNABLE PASTORAL REPENTANCE AND GROWTH

We should care about, pray for, and do all we can to work toward the constant, progressive spiritual growth of our pastors. We should not assume that it is taking place. We should want them in a thoroughly gospelized community that takes this seriously and invites them into loving, honest relationships where this kind of growth thrives. It is a very sad thing when a pastor moves from place of ministry to place of ministry and does not grow as the result of the things that a God of grace has exposed. Know this: if your eyes ever see or your ears ever hear the sin, weakness, or failure of your pastor, it should never be viewed as a hassle or an interruption; it is always grace. God loves that man and will expose his needs to you so that you can be part of his instrumentality of change and growth.

8) CARRYING PROBLEMS TO THE NEXT SITE OF MINISTRY

In the way that divorce often aborts the growth of a husband or a wife, the dissolving of a pastor's relationship to his church and the move to a new place of ministry often obstructs or inhibits his growth. There is often so much misunderstanding, back-and-forth accusation, and hurt that accompany this separation that it is very hard for the pastor to look at himself with the kind of objectivity and accuracy that is necessary for sightedness, conviction, and repentance. In fact, it is often worse than this. Often the pastor leaves convinced that his problem is not that he struggled with areas of sin but that he was naive enough to confess, and he silently determines he'll never put himself in this situation and do that again. I got push-back at an event, when I was doing this material, by a longtime pastor who was convinced that the only way for a pastor to survive is to live in silence and separation.

9) DISHONOR TO CHRIST'S NAME

This whole sad process denies the transforming power of the gospel, devalues the gifts Christ gives to his church, weakens the preaching of the gospel, diminishes the ministry of the church, and ultimately dishonors the name of Christ.

▲ ▲ ▲

Should we not work to build local-church cultures that encourage, require, and help pastors to be living examples of the heart- and life-transforming power of the gospel of Jesus Christ? Shouldn't we assume that the presence and power of remaining sin lives inside of every pastor? Should we not conclude, then, that it is dangerous for the pastor to live outside of the essential ministry of the body of Christ, which is there to guard, protect, confront, encourage, grow, and, if needed, restore him? Should we all not step back and ask heart-searching questions? If you are a pastor, do you live above or outside of the body of Christ? Do you seek out the insight-giving eyes and wisdom of others? Are there those who know you—I mean, really know you—at the level of the heart? Pastor, do you have a hunger to be pastored? If you are not a pastor, does your church do everything it can do to help your pastor benefit from the ministry of the body of Christ? Is he living in a gospel-centered culture of candor and love? Are you pastoring your pastor?

CHAPTER SEVEN

WAR ZONES

I guess it was the class I never took in seminary, but I had no concept of the battles I would face in ministry. Sure, I knew there would be battles for the gospel or battles for a biblical philosophy of ministry. I knew there would be skirmishes with fellow leaders or tugs of war between competing ministry interests. I knew that there would be an inevitable ebb and flow of ministry, that we would go through both bright and dark passages. I knew that people don't always hunger for or treasure the gospel of Jesus Christ as they should. I knew that not everyone to whom I was called to minister would have a natural affection for or connection to me. I knew I would be compared to the pastors who had preceded me. I knew that I would be called to minister in moments of meager resources of both help and money. I knew I would be called to battle for the gospel in people's lives in very hard moments. I knew that there would be times when people were angry with God and therefore not all that excited with me. I knew all of that, but what I didn't know or anticipate were the battles that would rage inside of me, battles that are unique to or intensified by pastoral ministry.

It's this inner war that I want to introduce in this chapter and that will make up the content of the rest of the book. As a pastor, you'd better be ready to fight for the gospel, but you'd better also be ready to war for your own soul. You'd better be committed to being honest about the battles that are going on in your own heart. You'd better be prepared to preach the gospel to yourself. You'd better arm yourself for the inner conflict that greets anyone in ministry.

MINISTRY IS WAR

Why do so many pastors report being overburdened and overstressed? Why do so many pastors report tension between family life and ministry life? Why does pastoral ministry often seem more of a trial than a joy? Why is there often disharmony between the private life of the pastor and his public ministry persona? Why are there often dysfunctional relationships between the pastor and his ministry leaders or staff? Why is the ministry life of many pastors shockingly short?

Perhaps we have forgotten that pastoral ministry is war and that you will never live successfully in the pastorate if you live with a peacetime mentality. Permit me to explain. The fundamental battle of pastoral ministry is not with the shifting values of the surrounding culture. It is not the struggle with resistant people who don't seem to esteem the gospel. It is not the fight for the success of the ministries of the church. And it is not the constant struggle of resources and personnel to accomplish the mission. No, the war of the pastorate is a deeply personal war. It is fought on the ground of the pastor's heart. It is a war of values, allegiances, and motivations. It is about subtle desires and foundational dreams. This war is the greatest threat to every pastor. Yet it is a war that we often naively ignore or quickly forget in the busyness of local-church ministry.

THE WAR FOR YOUR HEART

First, pastoral ministry is always shaped by a war between the kingdom of self and the kingdom of God, which is fought on the field of your heart. The reason this war is so dangerous and deceptive is that you build both kingdoms in ministry by doing ministry! Perhaps some theological background would be helpful here. Paul says in 2 Corinthians 5:15 that Jesus came so that those who live would no longer "live for themselves." Paul is arguing something significant here, something that every pastor should remember. He is arguing that the DNA of sin is selfishness. Sin inserts me into the middle of my universe, the one place reserved for God and God alone. Sin reduces my field of concern down to my wants, my needs, and my feelings. Sin really does make it all about me.

Because the inertia of sin leads away from God's purpose and glory toward my purpose and glory, as long as sin is inside of me there will be temptation to exchange God's glory for my own. In ways that are subtle and not so subtle, I begin to pursue the accoutrements of human glory. Things like appreciation, reputation, success, power, comfort, and control become all too important. Because they are too important to me, they begin to shape the way I think about ministry, the things I want out of my ministry, and the things I do in ministry. Remember, a pastor's ministry is not shaped just by his knowledge, gifts, skill, and experience but also by the condition of his heart. Could it be that much of the tension and despondency that pastors experience is the result of seeking to get things out of ministry that we should not be seeking?

WAR FOR THE GOSPEL

This leads us to a second battleground in the war that is pastoral ministry: the war for the gospel. Not only should we actively battle for the gospel as the fundamental paradigm for every ministry of the church, but we must also fight for the gospel to be the resting place of our hearts. Pastor, no one is more influential in your life than you are, because no one else talks to you more. The things you say to yourself about God, you, ministry, and others are profoundly important, shaping your participation in and experience of ministry. My experience with hundreds of pastors is that many sadly function in a regular state of *gospel amnesia*. They forget to preach privately to themselves the gospel that they declare publicly to others.

When you forget the gospel, you begin to seek from the situations, locations, and relationships of ministry what you have already been given in Christ. You begin to look to ministry for identity, security, hope, well-being, meaning, and purpose. These are things you will only ever find vertically. They are already yours in Christ. So you have to fight to give the gospel presence in your heart. Also, when you live out of the grace of the gospel, you quit fearing failure, you quit avoiding being known, and you quit hiding your struggles and your sin. The gospel declares that there is nothing that could ever be uncovered about you and me that hasn't already been covered by the grace of Jesus. The gospel is the only thing that can free a pastor from the guilt, shame, and drivenness of the *hide* ("never let your weakness show") and *seek* (asking ministry to do what Christ has already done) lifestyle that makes ministry burdensome to so many pastors.

So, in the war of pastoral ministry, are you a good soldier? Remember that the Holy Spirit lives inside of you, and he battles on your behalf even when you don't have the sense to. Remember too that in Christ you have already been given everything you need to be what you're supposed to be and to do what you're supposed to do in the place where God has positioned you. And remember that since Emmanuel is with you, it is impossible to ever be alone in the moment-by-moment war that is pastoral ministry.

TWO COMPETING KINGDOMS

It took God's employing pastoral hardship to get me to embrace the inescapable reality that everything I did in ministry was done in allegiance to and in pursuit of either the kingdom of self or the kingdom of God. This truth is best exegeted for us in Matthew 6:19–34. (Please grab your Bible and read the passage). I'm convinced that this passage is an elaborate unpacking of the thoughts, desires, and actions of the kingdom of self. Notice the turn in the passage in verse 33, where Jesus says, "But seek first the kingdom of God." The word "But" tells us this verse is the transition point of the passage. Everything before it explains the operation of another kingdom, the kingdom of self. This makes the passage a very helpful lens on the struggle between these two kingdoms that somehow, some way, battle in the heart of everyone in ministry.

In this chapter I want to examine from this passage four ministry treasure principles that I find helpful as I seek to examine the motivations of my own heart in ministry.

1) YOU WILL BE TREASURE ORIENTED IN YOUR MINISTRY.

We've been designed by God to be value-oriented, purpose-motivated beings. God gave us this capacity because he designed us for the worship of him. So what you do and say in ministry is always done in pursuit of some kind of treasure. I will explain later how few of the things that we treasure are intrinsically valuable. Most treasures have an assigned value. This side of eternity, here's what happens to all of us: things begin to rise in importance beyond their true importance and set the agenda for our thoughts, desires, choices, words, and actions.

What is the battle of treasure about? It is daily working to keep as important what God says is important in our personal lives and ministries. *Pastor, what is important to you in ministry?*

2) YOUR MINISTRY TREASURES WILL COMMAND THE ALLEGIANCE OF YOUR HEART.

Jesus says, "For where your treasure is, there your heart will be also" (v. 21). The heart, being the summary term for the inner man, could be characterized as the causal core of your personhood. What Jesus is saying here is profound. He's suggesting that there's a war of treasure being fought at the center of what makes you think what you think, desire what you desire, and do what you do. Whether you are conscious of it or not, your words and actions in ministry are always your attempt to get out of it what's valuable to you. *Pastor, what are the deep heart desires that shape your everyday words and actions?*

3) WHAT CAPTURES THE ALLEGIANCE OF YOUR HEART WILL SHAPE YOUR MINISTRY ACTIONS, REACTIONS, AND RESPONSES.

Remember that, by God's design, we're worshipers. Worship isn't first an activity; worship is first our identity. That means everything you and I do and say is the product of worship. So the treasures (things that have risen to levels of importance in our hearts) that rule the thoughts and desires of our hearts will then control the things that we do. The war between these two kingdoms in ministry is not first a war of behavior; it's a war for the functional, street-level rulership of our hearts. If we lose this deeper war, we'll never gain ground in the arena of our words and actions. *Pastor, what do your words and actions reveal about what's truly important to you?*

4) YOUR FUNCTIONAL TREASURES ARE ALWAYS ATTACHED TO EITHER THE KINGDOM OF SELF OR THE KINGDOM OF GOD.

Christ really does give us only two options. We attach our identity, meaning, purpose, and inner sense of well-being either to the earthbound treasures of the kingdom of self or to the heavenly treasures of the kingdom of God. This is an incredibly helpful diagnostic for pastoral ministry. Consider these questions: The absence of *what* causes us to want to give up and quit? The pursuit of *what* leads us to feeling overburdened and overwhelmed? The fear of *what* makes us tentative and timid rather than courageous and hopeful? The craving for *what* makes us burn the candle at both ends until we have little left? The "need" for *what* robs ministry of its beauty and joy? The desire for *what* sets up tensions between ministry and family?

▲ ▲ ▲

Could it be that many of the stresses of ministry are the result of our seeking to get things out of ministry that it will never deliver? Could it be that we're asking ministry to do for us what only the Messiah can do? Could it be that in our ministries we're seeking horizontally what we've already been given in Christ? Could it be that this kingdom conflict is propelled and empowered by functional, personal gospel amnesia? When we forget what we've been given in Christ, we tend to seek those things from the situations, locations, and relationships of our ministry. *Pastor, in what ways are you tempted to seek from your ministry what you've already been given in Christ?*

You see, the biggest protection against the kingdom of self is not a set of self-reformative defensive strategies. It's a heart that's so blown away by the right-here, right-now glories of the grace of Jesus Christ that we're not easily seduced by the lesser temporary glories of that claustrophobic kingdom of one, the kingdom of self. The problem is that no matter how committed we are to the big kingdom, we are always grappling with the dynamic of shifting treasure. Permit me to explain.

THE PROBLEM OF SHIFTING TREASURE

Let's begin by unpacking the concept of treasure that Christ uses. *Treasure* is a provocative word. Imagine I am holding a twenty-dollar bill in front of you. Why is it worth twenty dollars? It's not because it is made from twenty dollars' worth of paper. That would entail a stack of paper. It's not because it is made up of twenty dollars' worth of ink. That would entail a pail of ink. You see, the value of the twenty-dollar bill isn't intrinsic value but assigned value. Our government has assigned to that bill the value of two thousand pennies. Thus it is with most of the things that we treasure. Few of them have intrinsic value. No, most of them have assigned value. What does that mean? It means they have value because we have named them as valuable.

This is something you do all the time. You are constantly value-rating the things in your life. That's why the old proverb says, "One man's trash is another man's treasure." You are constantly naming things as important and other things as not so important. You are always attaching your inner hope and contentment to something, and when you do, those things take on life-shaping value.

Let's return to our twenty-dollar bill and see how it will shape our lives once that value has been assigned to it. Once my bill has the value of twenty dollars, the number of those you offer me will determine whether I will take that job or not. The number of those I have will determine the size of my house, the neighborhood I live in, the kind of car I drive, the quality of clothes I wear, the cuisine I eat, the level of health care I have, the vacations I take, and my hopes for retirement, and it may sadly even determine the kind of people I want to hang out with. Once something is our treasure, it will command our desires and shape our behavior.

So there are two practical conclusions that immediately flow from Christ's teaching on treasure. I want to state each conclusion in the context of pastoral ministry. *First, in pastoral ministry it is very hard to keep what God says is important, important in your heart.* What always happens to each one of us is that things in ministry rise in importance way beyond their true importance, and when they do, they begin to command our desires and shape our behavior. *Also, it is critical to understand that your ministry will always be either propelled by or victimized by what you treasure.* When you treasure what God says is truly valuable, your ministry will be protected and enhanced by the treasure commitments of your heart. But when you treasure things that God doesn't say are important, you find yourself in the way of, rather than part of, what God is doing in your ministry at that moment. Who in pastoral ministry cannot relate to the following example?

After the Sunday morning service he asked if he could make an appointment with me. I thought he had been touched by my sermon and wanted help in applying the truths to the details of his everyday life. What he actually wanted to do was tell me how bad—"painful" is what he actually said—my sermons were. He also said he was speaking for others who felt the same way. I was hurt, of course, but I went about preparing as I had the week before.

The next Sunday when I got up to preach and looked out at the listeners, everyone in the congregation had a normal-sized head except for this guy! His head seemed huge, with the eyes of the *Mona Lisa* that seemed to be staring at me from every angle. In ways I had been previously unaware, there had been a subtle shift in the motivation of my heart. Sure, I wanted to be faithful to the text and clearly explain the gospel, but I also wanted something else. I was determined to win this man. I was determined that he would come to me and say, "Paul, I was wrong; you really are a terrific preacher." I both prepared and communicated with him in mind.

The encroachment of the kingdom of self in ministry is really a matter of *shifting treasure.* Called to have everything I say and do ruled by the Christ-centered, grace-driven treasures of heaven, instead my ministry begins to be shaped by a catalog of earthbound treasures. My ministry begins to be shaped by subtle but formative shifts in the kind of treasure that rules my heart and, therefore, shapes my words and behavior. When things begin to control the thoughts and desires of my heart, they rise way beyond their true importance, and in so doing they shape the way I do ministry. Let me suggest just five of a long list of possible treasure shifts that can easily take place in the heart of any pastor.

1) IDENTITY: MOVING FROM IDENTITY IN CHRIST TO IDENTITY IN MINISTRY

In pastoral ministry, it is very tempting to look horizontally for what you have already been given in Christ. It is possible to be a pastor and a functional identity amnesiac. When I am, I begin to need my worth, inner sense of well-being, meaning, and purpose affirmed by the people and programs of the church. Rather than the hope and courage that come from resting in my identity in Christ, my ministry becomes captured and shaped by the treasure of a series of temporary horizontal affirmations of my value and worth. This robs me of ministry boldness and makes me all too focused on how those in the circle of my ministry are responding to me.

2) MATURITY: DEFINING SPIRITUAL WELL-BEING NOT BY THE MIRROR OF THE WORD BUT BY MINISTRY

Biblical literacy is not to be confused with Christian maturity. Homiletic accuracy is not the same as godliness. Theological dexterity is very different from practical holiness. Successful leadership is not the same as a heart for Christ. Growth in influence must not be confused with growth in grace. It is tempting to allow a shift to take place in the way that I evaluate my maturity as a pastor. Rather than living with a deep neediness for the continued operation of grace in my own heart, I begin, because of experience and success in ministry, to view myself as being more mature than I actually am. Because of these feelings of arrival, I don't sit under my own preaching; I don't preach out of a winsome, tender, and humble heart; and I don't seek out the ministry of the body of Christ. This allows my preparation to be less devotional and my view of others to be more judgmental.

3) REPUTATION: SHIFTING FROM A MINISTRY SHAPED BY ZEAL FOR THE REPUTATION OF CHRIST TO A MINISTRY SHAPED BY HUNGER FOR THE PRAISE OF PEOPLE

My ministry should be functionally motivated by the glory of Christ, that his fame would be known by more and more people, and that together we would all know practically what it means to submit to his lordship. Instead, my ministry becomes seduced by the treasure of my own reputation. My heart begins to be captured by the desire to be esteemed by others, the buzz of being needed, the allure of standing out in the crowd, the glory of being in charge, and the power of being right. This makes it hard to admit I am wrong, to submit to the counsel of others, to surrender control, to not have to win the day and prove I am right. It makes it hard to accept blame or to share credit, and it makes me less than excited about ministry as a body-of-Christ collaborative process.

4) ESSENTIALITY: MOVING FROM REST IN THE ESSENTIAL PRESENCE OF JESUS THE MESSIAH TO SEEING ONESELF AS WAY TOO ESSENTIAL TO WHAT GOD IS DOING

Where once I viewed myself as one of many tools in God's kingdom toolbox, I now begin to see myself as too central, too important to what God is doing in my local setting. Rather than resting in the person and work of the Messiah, I begin to load the burden of the individual and collective growth of God's people onto my own shoulders. This causes me to devalue the importance of the gifts and ministry of others and tempts me to assign to myself more than I am able to do. In ways that I probably am not aware of, I've begun to try to be the Messiah instead of resting in my identity as a tool in his faithful and powerful hands.

5) CONFIDENCE: SHIFTING AWAY FROM A HUMBLE CONFIDENCE IN TRANSFORMING GRACE TO OVERCONFIDENCE IN ONE'S OWN EXPERIENCE AND GIFTS

Longevity and success in ministry are good things, but they can also be dangerous things for the heart of a pastor. We are all capable of becoming all too confident in ourselves. A confidence shift begins to take place from the treasure of humble confidence in the power of rescuing, forgiving, transforming, and delivering grace, to rest in my own knowledge, abilities, gifts, and experience. Because of this, I don't grieve enough, I don't pray enough, I don't prepare enough, I don't confess enough, and I don't listen to others enough. I have begun to assign to myself capabilities I don't have, and because I do,

I don't minister out of my own sense of need for Christ's grace, and I don't seek out the help of others.

▲ ▲ ▲

In each area it is tempting for my ministry to be shaped by a shift from confidence in the treasure of the relentless grace of Jesus, the redeemer, to hope in earthbound treasures, which he reminds us (Matt. 6:19–34) are temporary by nature and have no capacity to deliver what we are seeking. Could it be that these treasure shifts lead to so many of the familiar institutional problems and relational breakdowns in ministry? Could it be that these shifts are what cause ministry to become a burden rather than the joy that it actually is? Your ministry will live at the dangerous intersection between the difficulties and temptations of this fallen world and the kingdom battle that is still going on in your heart. This crucial intersection will be the focus of the rest of this book.

The treasures of the kingdom of self become all the more seductive and powerful when I, as pastor, lose sight of the glories of what I've been given in Christ. When I do this, I begin to think of myself as poor when grace has made me rich, and I seek riches in places where they simply cannot be found. But I need not run away in shame or give way to panic, because the grace of the cross has covered this struggle as well and will work again today to rescue me from me.

WHAT TO REMEMBER

In the face of all of this, what are the things that we must remember? Let's approach the question this way. The experts say that there are only three things to consider when buying a piece of property: location, location, location. The same could be said about life. When you understand location, you live and minister in a radically different way. Confused? Let me point you to four ways in which location matters.

1) YOU LIVE IN A DRAMATICALLY FALLEN WORLD.

You have to be prepared. You have to live with realistic expectations. You simply must bring a biblical understanding to the place where you now live and minister, or you will be constantly unprepared and disappointed. You and I live in a very broken world where there is trouble on every side. Your body and mind are affected by the fall and don't always work as they should. Your family and friendships will not work as they were designed. The government over you does not function as it was created to function. The church you serve is filled with flawed people yet in need of redemption. The broken physical environment suffers under the weight of the fall. The apostle Paul says it very well in Romans 8: "The whole creation has been groaning together in the pains of childbirth until now. And not only the creation, but we ourselves, who have the firstfruits of the Spirit, groan inwardly as we wait eagerly for adoption as sons, the redemption of our bodies" (vv. 22–24).

There's no escaping it: you are located in a place where trouble of some kind will greet you every day. Much of that trouble will live inside you. You live and minister in a place where somehow, some way, temptation will greet you every day. When you face this harsh reality, you will live prepared for the troubles that come your way.

2) THE BIG BATTLE IS FOUGHT IN YOUR HEART.

In acknowledging the brokenness of the world where you live and minister, you do not want to give way to spiritual environmentalism in which you blame all of your struggles on things outside of you. That was the mistake of the medieval monastery, walled communities separated from the evil world and intended to foster righteous living. As it turned out, these communities tended to repeat all the ills of the surrounding world from which they had separated.

Monasteries were a failure because they neglected one very significant biblical truth: the biggest danger to every human being, even those in ministry, is located inside of him, not outside of him. There is something dark and deceitful that still lurks in the heart of every one of God's children who has not yet been fully glorified: sin. It is only ever the sin inside of you that draws and hooks you to the sin outside of you. Every day there is a war fought for control of your heart. But your jealous Savior, with the zeal of gorgeous redemptive love, will not share your heart. He will not rest until your heart is ruled by him and him alone.

3) YOU WILL RUN SOMEWHERE FOR REFUGE.

In the middle of trouble, when you are in the heat of the battle, you will run somewhere for refuge. You will run somewhere for rest, comfort, peace, encouragement, wisdom, healing, and strength. There is only one place to run where true protection, rest, and strength can be found. You and I must learn, in life and ministry, to make the Lord our refuge.

Perhaps in trouble you run to other people, hoping that they can be your personal messiah. Perhaps you run to entertainment, hoping to numb your troubles away. Maybe you run to a substance, trying your best to turn off the pain. Maybe you are tempted to run to food or sex, fighting pain with pleasure. Since none of these things can provide the refuge that you seek, putting your hope there tends only to add disappointment to the trouble you're already experiencing.

God really is your refuge and strength. Only he rules every location where your trouble exists. Only he controls all the relationships in which disappointment will rear its head. Only he has the power to rescue and deliver you. Only he has the grace you need to face what you are facing. Only he holds the wisdom that, in trouble, you so desperately need. Only he is in, with, and for you at all times. He is the refuge of refuges. Do you run to him?

4) WHERE YOU ARE HEADING, TROUBLE WILL BE NO MORE.

You could argue that the biblical story is about three locations. The garden in Genesis was a location of perfection and beauty but became a place of sin and trouble. The hill of Calvary was a place of both horrible suffering and transforming grace. And the New Jerusalem, that place of peace and refuge lit by the brightness of the Son, will be our final refuge forever. Because of the cross of Jesus Christ, your story will not end with daily trouble and temporary refuge. No, your final location will be utterly unlike anything you have ever experienced, even on your best and brightest ministry day. You are headed for the New Jerusalem, where the final tear will be dried and trouble will be no more.

▲ ▲ ▲

Today, in life and ministry, you will face trouble of some kind. Today you will run somewhere for refuge. Today there is hope and help to be found. May God be your refuge, and as you run to him, may you remember that he has promised you that there will be a day when your trouble is no more. But you live between the already and the not yet, and the battle still rages. The question for you, pastor, is, are you an aware, wise, and prepared soldier who runs again and again to the Captain of your soul for rescuing, forgiving, transforming, empowering, and delivering grace?

PART 2

THE DANGER OF LOSING YOUR AWE

(FORGETTING WHO GOD IS)

CHAPTER EIGHT

FAMILIARITY

He said it rather matter-of-factly, probably not understanding the significance of what he was saying, but I couldn't get his words out of my head. He was the head of a national ministry. We were in a meeting, talking about ministry partnership. I was sharing my excitement about what I saw happening in the church around the world, and he said, "I don't think anything excites me anymore." It wasn't my place to respond to what he said, but I immediately thought, *You'd better be excited. You are leading a ministry, and if you can't get your excitement back, maybe you shouldn't be doing what you're doing.* He had lost his excitement, and he was left with a duty to do the business of ministry in repetitive, day-after-day, joyless obligation. What a sad and dangerous place to be!

Perhaps it begins in seminary with the up-close examination of every element of the faith. Perhaps there is a moment when the glory of God just doesn't seem all that glorious anymore. Perhaps living in the middle of a theological community begins to dull my excitement and numb my amazement. Perhaps the Bible gets reduced to little more than a theological manual to be exegeted and responded to. Perhaps even God himself becomes more a divine being to study and theologically understand than the Lord of glory that he is.

Perhaps it is all about the dynamic of familiarity. The great Princeton professor and theologian B. B. Warfield wrote this to his students:

> We are frequently told, indeed, that the great danger of the theological student lies precisely in his constant contact with divine things. They may come to seem common to him because they are customary. As the average man breathes the air and basks in the

> sunshine without ever a thought that it is God in his goodness who makes his sun to rise on him, though he is evil, and sends rain to him, though he is unjust; so you may come to handle even the furniture of the sanctuary with never a thought above the gross earthly materials of which it is made. The words which tell you of God's terrible majesty or of his glorious goodness may come to be mere words to you—Hebrew and Greek words, with etymologies, inflections and connections in sentences. The reasonings which establish to you the mysteries of his saving activities may come to be to you mere logical paradigms, with premises and conclusions, fitly framed, no doubt, and triumphantly cogent, but with no further significance to you than their formal logical conclusiveness. God's stately steppings in his redemptive processes may become to you a mere series of facts of history, curiously interplaying to the production of social and religious conditions and pointing mayhap to an issue which we may shrewdly conjecture: but much like other facts occurring in time and space which may come to your notice. It is your great danger. But it is your great danger *only* because it is your great privilege. Think of what your privilege is when your greatest danger is that the great things of religion may become common to you! Other men, oppressed by the hard conditions of life, sunk in the daily struggle for bread perhaps, distracted at any rate by the dreadful drag of the world upon them and the awful rush of the world's work, find it hard to get time and opportunity so much as to pause and consider whether there be such things as God, and religion, and salvation from the sin that compasses them about and holds them captive. The very atmosphere of your life is these things; you breathe them in at every pore: they surround you, encompass you, press in upon you from every side. It is all in danger of becoming common to you! God forgive you, you are in danger of becoming weary of God![*]

What powerful words of warning to everyone in ministry of any type: "The great danger . . . lies precisely in his constant contact with divine things." What is the danger? It is that familiarity with the things of God will cause you to lose your awe. You've spent so much

[*]Benjamin B. Warfield, "The Religious Life of Theological Students," from an address delivered by Warfield at the Autumn Conference at Princeton Theological Seminary, October 4, 1911.

time in Scripture that its grand redemptive narrative, with its expansive wisdom, doesn't excite you anymore. You've spent so much time exegeting the atonement that you can stand at the foot of the cross with little weeping and scant rejoicing. You've spent so much time discipling others that you are no longer amazed at the reality of having been chosen to be a disciple of Jesus Christ. You've spent so much time unpacking the theology of Scripture that you've forgotten that its end game is personal holiness. You've spent so much time in strategic, local-church ministry planning that you've lost your wonder at the sovereign Planner that guides your every moment. You've spent so much time meditating on what it means to lead others in worship, but you have little private awe. It's all become so regular and normal that it fails to move you anymore; in fact, there are sad moments when the wonder of grace can barely get your attention in the midst of your busy ministry schedule.

Artists talk of the dynamic of visual lethargy, which means that the more you see something, the less you actually *see* it. On that drive to work the first day, you are conscious of all the sights and sounds. You notice that beautiful grove of ancient trees and that cool modern duplex on the corner. But by your twentieth trip, you've quit noticing, and you're wishing the traffic would move faster so you could get to work, for Pete's sake! Something has happened to you that seems inevitable but is not good. You have quit seeing, and in your failure to see, you have quit being moved and thankful. The beauty that once attracted you is still there to see, but you don't see it, and you cannot celebrate what you fail to see. Could there be a greater danger in ministry than that the one leading the ministry would lose his awe? Let me explain.

Perhaps the place to begin is with one of the Bible's awe passages, Psalm 145.

> I will extol you, my God and King,
>   and bless your name forever and ever.
> Every day I will bless you
>   and praise your name forever and ever.

Great is the LORD, and greatly to be praised,
and his greatness is unsearchable.

One generation shall commend your works to another,
and shall declare your mighty acts.
On the glorious splendor of your majesty,
and on your wondrous works, I will meditate.
They shall speak of the might of your awesome deeds,
and I will declare your greatness.
They shall pour forth the fame of your abundant goodness
and shall sing aloud of your righteousness.

The LORD is gracious and merciful,
slow to anger and abounding in steadfast love.
The LORD is good to all,
and his mercy is over all that he has made.

All your works shall give thanks to you, O LORD,
and all your saints shall bless you!
They shall speak of the glory of your kingdom
and tell of your power,
to make known to the children of man your mighty deeds,
and the glorious splendor of your kingdom.
Your kingdom is an everlasting kingdom,
and your dominion endures throughout all generations.

The LORD is faithful in all his words
and kind in all his works.
The LORD upholds all who are falling
and raises up all who are bowed down.
The eyes of all look to you,
and you give them their food in due season.
You open your hand;
you satisfy the desire of every living thing.
The LORD is righteous in all his ways
and kind in all his works.
The LORD is near to all who call on him,
to all who call on him in truth.
He fulfills the desire of those who fear him;

> he also hears their cry and saves them.
> The LORD preserves all who love him,
> but all the wicked he will destroy.
>
> My mouth will speak the praise of the LORD,
> and let all flesh bless his holy name forever and ever.

What is the overriding worldview of this psalm? It is that every human being has been hardwired by God to live in daily awe of him. This means the deepest, most life-shaping, practical daily motivation of every human being was designed to be the awe of God. This is the calling of every person. This is the umbrella of protection over every person. This is the reality that is to define and give shape to every other reality in a person's life. What does this functionally look like?

Well, it should be the thing that in some way motivates everything I do and say. Awe of God should be the reason I do what I do with my thoughts. It should be the reason I desire what I desire. Awe of God should be the reason I treat my wife the way I do and parent my children in the manner I do. It should be the reason I function the way I do at my job or handle my finances the way I do. It should structure the way I think about physical possession and personal position and power. Awe of God should shape and motivate my relationship with my extended family and neighbors. Awe of God should give direction to the way I live as a citizen of the wider community. It should form the way that I think about myself and my expectations of others. Awe of God should lift me out of my darkest moments of discouragement and be the source of my most exuberant celebrations. Awe of God should make me more self-aware and more mournful of my sin while it makes me more patient with and tender toward the weakness of others. It should give me courage I would have no other way and wisdom to know when I am out of my league. Awe of God is meant to rule every domain of my existence.

But there is more. Awe of God must dominate my ministry, because one of the central missional gifts of the gospel of Jesus Christ is to give people back their awe of God. A human being who is not living in a functional awe of God is a profoundly disadvantaged human being. He is off the rails, trying to propel the train of his life in a meadow, and he may not even know it. The spiritual danger here is that when awe of God is absent, it is quickly replaced by our awe of ourselves. If you are not living for God, the only alternative is to live for yourself. So a central ministry of the church must be to do anything it can to be used of God to turn people back to the one thing for which they were created: to live in a sturdy, joyful, faithful awe of God.

This means that every sermon should be prepared by a person whose study is marked by awe of God. The sermon must be delivered in awe and have as its purpose to motivate awe in those who hear. Children's ministry must have as its goal to ignite in young children a life-shaping awe of God. The youth ministry of the church must move beyond Bible entertainment and do all it can to help teens to see God's glory and name it as the thing for which they will live. Women's ministry must do more than give women a place to fellowship with one another and do crafts. Women need to be rescued from themselves and a myriad of self-interests that nip at their hearts, and awe of God provides that rescue. Men's ministries need to recognize the coldness in the heart of so many men to the things of God and confront and stimulate men with their identity as those created to live and lead out of a humble zeal for God's glory rather than their own. Missions and evangelism must be awe-driven. Remember, Paul argues that this is the reason for the cross. He says that Jesus came so that "those who live may no longer live for themselves, but for him who loved them and gave himself for them" (see 2 Cor. 5:15).

Awe of God is one of the things that will keep a church from running off its rails and being diverted by the many agendas that can sidetrack any congregation. Awe of God puts theology in its place. Theology is vitally important, but whatever awe of theology we have is dangerous if it doesn't produce in us a practical awe of God. Awe of God puts the ministry strategies of the church in their proper place. We don't put our trust in our strategies but in the God of awesome glory, who is the head of the church we are endeavoring to lead well.

Awe of God puts ministry gifts and experience in their proper place. We cannot grow arrogant and smug about our gifts, because unless those gifts are empowered by the glorious grace of the God we serve, they have no power to rescue or change anyone. Awe of God puts our music and liturgy in its proper place. Yes, we should want to lead people in worship that is both biblical and engaging, but we have no power to really engage the heart of people without the awesome presence of the Holy Spirit, who propels and applies all we seek to do. Awe of God puts our buildings and property in their proper place. How a building is constructed, maintained, and used is a very important issue, but buildings have never called or justified anyone; only a God of awesome sovereign grace is able to do so. Awe of God puts our history and traditions in their proper place. Yes, we should be thankful for the ways God has worked in our past, and we should seek to retain the things that are a proper expression of what he says is important, but we don't rest in our history; we rest in the God of glory, who is the same yesterday, today, and forever!

We must be committed to do anything we can to be that generation that commends God's works, his glory, to the next generation so that they may be rescued and motivated by a glory bigger than the typical catalog of glories they would choose for themselves.

Now, it's very hard to preach and shape the ministry of the church this way if familiarity has produced a blindness that has effectively robbed you of your awe of God. It is very difficult in ministry to give away what you do not possess yourself (a major theme of this book). In ways of which you are not always aware, your ministry is always shaped by what is in functional control of your heart. If you are more motivated by the awe-inspiring experience of having the esteem and respect of the people around you, you will do ministry in a way that is structured to get that respect, even though you probably aren't aware of it. If your heart is ruled by the awesome power that comes from controlling the people and situations around you, you will work in your ministry to be in control. If your heart is more ruled by fear of man than by fear of God, you will build a ministry that erects walls of protection around you and builds a moat between your public persona and your private life. If your heart is more moved by the awe-stimulating experience of being theologically right than by an awe of God, who lives at the center of all that theology, you will be a theological gatekeeper who does not pastor messy people well. If your heart is ruled more by envy over the awe-inspiring ministry of another than by an awe of the God who has called and gifted you, you will minister out of a debilitating dissatisfaction with the situation and location of your calling.

Remember again that the ministry you are doing is never just shaped by your gifts, knowledge, skill, and experience. It is always also shaped by the true condition of your heart. This is why it is important to acknowledge that local church ministry is one big glory war. In every situation, location, and relationship of your ministry there is a war going on for what glory will magnetize your heart and, therefore, shape your ministry. There is a war going on between the awe of God and all of the awe-inspiring things that are around you that God created. Awe of God will capture you and your ministry, or you will be captured by some kind of created awe. Remember, any glorious thing in creation was given that glory by God so it would function as a finger pointing you to the one glory that should rule your heart—him.

The fact of the matter is that many pastors become awe numb or awe confused, or they get awe kidnapped. Many pastors look at glory and don't see glory anymore. Many pastors are just cranking out because they don't know what else to do. Many pastors preach a boring, uninspiring gospel that makes you wonder why more people aren't sleeping their way through it. Many pastors are better at arguing fine points of doctrine than at stimulating divine wonder. Many pastors seem more stimulated by the next ministry vision or the next step in the strategic plan than by the stunning glory of the grand intervention of grace into sin-broken hearts. The glories of being right, successful, in control, esteemed, and secure often become more influential in the way that ministry is done than the awesome realities of the presence, sovereignty, power, and love of God. Many pastors have lost their awe and either don't know it or don't know how to get it back.

THE PRACTICAL MINISTRY FRUIT OF THE AWE OF GOD

What things does the awe of God produce in the heart of a pastor that are vital for an effective, God-honoring, and productive ministry? Below is your list.

1) HUMILITY

There is nothing that will put you in your place, nothing that will correct your distorted view of yourself, nothing that will yank you out of your functional arrogance, or nothing that will take the winds out of the sails of your self-righteousness like standing, without defense, before the awesome glory of God.

In the face of his glory I am left naked with no glory whatsoever to hold before myself or anyone else. As long as I am comparing myself to others, I can always find someone whose existence seems to be an argument for how righteous I am. But if I compare the filthy rags of my righteousness to the pure and forever unstained linen of God's righteousness, I want to run and hide in heartbreaking shame.

This is exactly what happened to Isaiah, recorded in Isaiah 6. He stands before the awesome throne of God's glory and says, "Woe is me! For I am lost; for I am a man of unclean lips, and I dwell in the midst of a people of unclean lips; for my eyes have seen the King, the Lord of hosts!" (v. 5). Isaiah is not speaking in formal religious hyperbole here. He is not trying to ingratiate himself with God by being oh so humble. No, it is only in light of the awesome glory and holiness of God that you come to have an accurate view of yourself and the depth of your need for the rescue that only a God of glorious grace can provide.

Somewhere along the way in ministry, too many pastors have forgotten who they are. They have a bloated, distorted, grandiose view of themselves that renders them largely unapproachable and allows them to justify things they think, desire, say, and do that simply are not biblically justifiable. I have been there and at times fall into being there again, and when I am there, I need to be rescued from me. When you are too much in awe of you, you set up to be a self-righteous, controlling, overconfident, judgmental, unfalteringly opinionated, ecclesiastical autocrat, unwittingly building a kingdom whose throne will be inhabited by you, no matter how much you are able to convince yourself that you do it all for the glory of God.

2) TENDERNESS

The humility that awe of God is alone able to produce in my heart—that is, an awareness of my sin and desperate need for grace—then produces pastoral tenderness toward the people around me, who give empirical evidence that they are in need of the same grace. No one gives grace better than a person who is deeply persuaded that he needs it himself and is being given it in Christ. This tenderness causes me to be gracious, gentle, patient, understanding, and hopeful in the face of the sin of others, while never compromising God's holy call. It protects me from deadly assessments like, "I can't believe you would do such a thing," or, "I would never have thought of . . . ," that are me telling me that I am essentially different from the people to whom I minister. It's hard to bring the gospel to people I am looking down my nose at or neither like nor respect. In the face of the sin of others, awe-inspired tenderness frees me from being an agent of condemnation or from asking the law to do what only grace can accomplish and motivates me to be a tool of that grace.

3) PASSION

No matter what is or isn't working in my ministry, no matter what difficulties or battles I am facing, the expansive glory of God gives me reason to get up in the morning and do what I have been gifted and called to do with enthusiasm, courage, and confidence. My joy isn't handcuffed to the surrounding circumstances or relationships; I don't have to have my heart yanked wherever they go. I have reason for joy because I am a chosen child and a conscripted servant of the King of kings and Lord of lords, the great Creator, the Savior, the sovereign, the victor, the one who does reign and will reign forever. He is my Father, my Savior, and my boss. He is ever near and ever faithful.

My passion for ministry is not about how I am being received; it flows out of the reality that I have been received by him. My enthusiasm is not because people like me, but because he has accepted and sent me. My passion is not the result of my ministry being as glorious as I thought it could be, but because he is eternally and unchangeably glorious. So I preach, teach, counsel, lead, and serve with a gospel passion that inspires and ignites the same in the people around me.

4) CONFIDENCE

The confidence, that inner sense of well-being and capability in ministry, is not untoward self-confidence but comes from a knowledge of whom I serve. He is my confidence and ability. He will not call me to a task without enabling me to do it. He has more zeal for the health of his church than I ever will. No one has more interest in the use of my gifts than the one who gave them. No one has more zeal for his glory than he does. He is ever-present and ever-willing. He is all-powerful and all-knowing. He is boundless in love and glorious in grace. He does not change, and he is faithful forever. His word will not cease to be true. His power to save will never be exhausted. His rule will not run out. He will never be conquered by one greater than he. I can do what I have been called to do with confidence, not because of who I am but because he is my Father, and he is glorious in every way.

5) DISCIPLINE

There are inglorious times in everyone's ministry. There are times when the naive expectations you have had of what it all would be like have proven to be just that—naive. There are passages of time when it's going to take more than ministry success and the appreciation of the people around you to pull you out of bed to do with discipline the things you have been called to do. There will be times when there seems to be little fruit as the result of your labors and little hope of that changing anytime soon. There are times when you will think you have been betrayed and you feel alone. So it is vital that your discipline is rooted in something deeper than a horizontal assessment of how things are going. I am more and more persuaded in my own life that sturdy self-discipline, the kind that is essential in pastoral ministry, is rooted in worship. It is the awesome glory of God's existence, character, plan, presence, promises, and grace that gives me reason to work hard and not give up, no matter whether we are in a "good" season or one that is stormy.

6) REST

Finally, as I face my own weaknesses and the messiness of the local church, what gives me rest of heart? It is glory that gives me rest. It is the knowledge that there is nothing too hard for the God whom I serve. It is the surety that all things are possible with him. It is knowing, with Abraham, that the One who made all those promises on which I base my ministry is faithful. There may seem to be many horizontal reasons to be anxious, but I will not let my heart be captured by worry or fear, because the God of inestimable glory who sent me has made this promise: "I will be with you." I don't have to play games with myself. I don't have to deny or minimize reality in order to feel okay, because he has invaded my existence with his glory, and I can rest, even in the brokenness between the already and the not yet.

▲ ▲ ▲

GETTING YOUR AWE BACK

I don't have a set of strategies for you here. My counsel is to run now, run quickly, to your Father of awesome glory. Confess the offense of your boredom. Plead for eyes that are open to the 360-degree, 24/7 display of glory to which you have been blind. Determine to spend a certain portion of every day in meditating on his glory. Cry out for the help of others. And remind yourself to be thankful for Jesus, who offers you his grace even at those moments when that grace isn't nearly as valuable to you as it should be.

CHAPTER NINE

DIRTY SECRETS

He got used to the bad habits of unfaith. "They're just my way of unwinding," he'd tell himself. He reasoned that they didn't get in the way of what he had been called to do. He kept telling himself that he was working hard and doing well, but he wasn't doing well. He had more sleepless nights than he was ready to admit. He had gained thirty pounds over the last several years. He numbed his brain every night with hours upon hours of vacuous TV or Internet pop culture. He had incurred more debt than ever before in his life. His wife would have said that he had become increasingly irritable and distant. At home he often came across as a rather joyless, overburdened man. His kids would say that even when he was there, he was often "not there." He dreaded meetings and found himself easily distracted when he needed focus in order to prepare his next sermon. The door to his office was shut more now than it had been, and he delegated more of his duties to his executive pastor.

Yet no one in the congregation had a clue. He did all his public duties, and from the perspective of the person in the pew, he seemed to do them rather well. He led the meetings that he was appointed to lead and did his best to do the follow-up work that landed on his desk. The problem was that he was not doing well. There was a growing disparity between the public persona and the private man. There was a growing disconnect between the faith statements he made from up front and the thinking that ruled his heart most of the time. He carried around with him the dirty secret that many pastors carry, the one that is so hard for a "man of faith" to admit. The dirty secret was that much of what he did was not done out of faith but out of fear.

Perhaps this is a not-too-often-shared secret of pastoral ministry; that is, how much of it is driven not by faith in the truths of the gospel and in the person and work of the Lord Jesus Christ but by fear. It is very tempting for the pastor to load the welfare of the church on his shoulders, and when he does, he ends up being burdened and motivated by an endless and ever-changing catalog of "what ifs." This never leads to a restful and joyful life of ministry but rather to a ministry debilitated by unrealistic and unmet goals, a personal sense of failure, and the dread that results.

How many pastors are living in a constant state of spiritual unrest? How many of us are haunted by personal insecurity? How many of us secretly wonder where God is and what in the world he is doing? How many of us are living self-protectively, saying, "I was taken once; it won't happen to me again"? How many of us are afraid to admit failure? How many of us share with no one the struggles of faith that haunt us? How many of us fail to be candid and decisive because we are afraid of what will happen if we do? How many of us have found ways of escape, ways of coping that do not include preaching the gospel to ourselves? How many of us wish for easier places of ministry? How many of us carry our burdens home, rendering our parenting less than gracious and productive? How many of us have become quite skilled at hiding so that not even the people closest to us have any sense of what is going on at the level of our hearts? How many of us have moments of compromise fueled by the fear of man? How many of us have given particular people too much power of influence over us? How many of us have let fear cause us to be too opinionated, too domineering, and too controlling? How many of us let fear keep us silent when we ought to speak or drive us to speak when we ought to be silent? How many of us regularly work to recast as acts of faith things that we have actually done out of fear? How many of us would have to confess that there are moments when we are more ruled by fear of ________ than fear of God? How many of us have moments when we care more about being accepted or having our leadership validated than we do about being biblical? How many of us are weakened or paralyzed by fear of rejection? How many of us are too fearful to entrust vital pieces of the ministry of our churches to others? How many of us are afraid to examine how much fear engages and motivates us? How many of us?

LET'S TALK ABOUT FEAR

1) IN A FALLEN WORLD THERE ARE REASONS TO BE AFRAID.

We live in a fallen, sin-broken world that does not operate as God intended. Whether it's the weeds that tangle your garden, the violence that makes the inner city dangerous, the corruption of the city politician, or the death of a loved one, there are plenty of reminders all around you that the world in which we live is broken. Because of this, we all live and minister in an unpredictable and dangerous place where unforeseen, difficult things do happen. Your salvation and your call to ministry do not automatically give you a ticket out of the fallenness of your surroundings. Your life and your ministry will be touched and in some way shaped by the brokenness of your world. Whether it's the downturn of the economy, the adultery of an elder, unexpected physical sickness, or some other trial, you will face hardship.

Because of this, it is silly to live in a fallen world and not be afraid in the responsible sense of what that means. Biblical faith does not require you to deny reality, so there are things that should concern and sober you. There are things that should cause you grief. There are things that you will be called to deal with quickly and decisively because of their potential danger. There are moments when fear of what could be is a spiritually healthy thing, but what you must guard against is being ruled by fear. The directive of Psalm 37:8 is very helpful here: "Fret not yourself; it tends only to evil." If you allow yourself to be ruled by fear, you will trouble your own trouble. You will end up making bad things worse. The decisions we make in the panic of fear are the ones we end up regretting.

2) IN RELATIONSHIPS WITH FLAWED PEOPLE, THERE ARE REASONS TO BE AFRAID.

Everyone you minister with and to is a flawed human being still in need of redemption. No one around you has a completely pure heart.

No one is totally free of sinful thoughts, desires, cravings, or motives. No one always says the right thing. No one always makes the right choices. No one is always noble in his intentions. No one is free from acts of selfishness or self-aggrandizement. No one is completely loyal. No one always has your back. Because of this, relationships in the body of Christ are messy and unpredictable. They are the places where we experience some of our most gratifying joys and heart-wrenching pains. It is godly and responsible to be afraid of how sin can create power struggles, divisive ally groups, critical and judgmental attitudes, self-centered complaining, disloyalty, and ultimately division.

3) FEAR CAN BE A VERY GOOD AND GODLY THING.

There is fear that causes you to be watchful and to protect the people in your ministry from the dangers of the real evil that exists both inside and outside of them. Eyes-wide-open, gospel-driven, sin-warring fear that at the same time rests in the grace of Jesus is a very good way to live in a world that itself is still groaning, waiting for redemption.

4) FEAR CAN BE AN UNGODLY AND DANGEROUS THING.

Fear can overwhelm your senses. It can distort your thinking. It can kidnap your desires. It can capture your meditation so that you spend more time worrying about what others think than about what God has called you to be. Fear can cause you to make bad decisions quickly and fail to make good decisions in the long run. Fear can cause you to forget what you know and to lose sight of who you are. Fear can make you wish for control that you will never have. It can cause you to distrust people you have reason to trust. It can cause you to be demanding rather than serving. It can cause you to run when you should stay and to stay when you really should run. Fear can make God look small and your circumstance loom large. Fear can make you seek from people what you will only get from the Lord. Fear can be the soil of your deepest questions and your biggest doubts. Your heart was wired to fear, because you were designed to have a life that is shaped by fear of God. But horizontal fear cannot be allowed to rule your heart, because if it does, it will destroy you and your ministry.

5) FEAR IS ONLY EVER CONQUERED BY FEAR.

Awe of God really is the solution here. It is only fear of God that has the spiritual power to overwhelm all the horizontal fears that can capture your heart. These relational-situational-location fears are only ever put in their proper place and given their appropriate size by a greater fear—fear of the Lord. Perhaps this is a good portion of what is being said in Proverbs when it declares that "fear of the LORD is the beginning of wisdom" (9:10). Allowing yourself to be twisted and turned by whatever fear has you at the moment is an unwise, unstable, and unproductive way of living. Living just to alleviate fear never leads to being fear free. It simply makes you more fearful of fear, more fear alert, and ultimately more fearful. It is only when God looms larger than anything you are facing that you can be protected and practically freed from the fear that either paralyzes you or causes you to make foolish decisions. Wise, stable, and fear-free living doesn't require you to deny what you're facing, but rather looks at whatever you are facing from the perspective of a gloriously freeing and motivating fear of the One who rules all the things that you would otherwise be afraid of. A functional awe of God really is the key to your heart's not being ruled by fear.

FOUR DEBILITATING PASTORAL FEARS

1) FEAR OF ME

There are few things that will reveal to you the full range of your sin, immaturity, weakness, and failure like ministry will. There are few things that will expose your weaknesses to others as consistently as ministry does. There are few endeavors that will put you under public expectancy and scrutiny like ministry does. There are few things that are as personally humbling as ministry is. There are few endeavors that have the power to produce in you such deep feelings of inadequacy as ministry does. There are few things that can be such a vat of self-doubt as ministry is. In your ministry there is a great temptation to be sidetracked and harmed by your fear of you.

God finds Gideon threshing wheat in a winepress, because he was afraid of the Midianites, and greets this fearful man with one of the most ironic greetings in the Bible: "The Lord is with you, O mighty man of valor" (Judg. 6:12). Gideon essentially replies, "Well, if you're with us, why is all this bad stuff happening?" God says, "I have chosen you to save Israel from the Midianites." Gideon says, "You have to have the wrong address. I am from the weakest clan in Israel and I am the weakest person in my father's house. You can't really mean me." And God says, "I will be with you."

God's response to Gideon's fear of Gideon is very helpful here. He didn't work to pump up his self-confidence. He didn't work to help Gideon see that he brought more to the table than he thought he did. He didn't do that, because Gideon's problem was not first that he feared his inadequacies. No, his problem was an awe problem. Gideon failed to fear God in the "God is with me and he is able" sense of what that means. So Gideon was terrified at the thought of leading Israel anywhere.

My pastorate in Scranton, Pennsylvania, had been successful in exposing the full range of my immaturity and weakness, and in ways that had been very painful these were often on public display. I had thought I was so ready. I had done very well in seminary, and I was ready to take on the world. But God had called me to a very broken, very difficult place and had used this place to yank me out of my pride and self-righteousness so that I would find my hope in him. I was hurt, disappointed, tired, overwhelmed, angry, and a bit bitter. I felt God had set me up and people had treated me unkindly, and all I wanted to do was run. I had an education degree and thought I would move somewhere far away and run a Christian school. I had announced my plan to resign to my board. They pleaded with me not to go, but I was determined. So the next Sunday I made my announcement and had a momentary sense of relief. Well, my little congregation was not relieved, so I had many conversations after the service. Much later than usual I made my way out the door, only to be greeted by the oldest man in our church.

He approached me and asked if we could talk. "Paul," he said, "we know that you're a bit immature and need to grow up. We know you are a man with weaknesses, but where is the church going to get mature pastors if immature pastors leave?" I felt as if God had just nailed my shoes to the porch. I knew he was right, and I knew I couldn't leave. In the next several months I began to learn what it means to minister in weakness but with a security-giving, courage-producing awe of God. I am still learning what it means to be in such awe of him that I am no longer afraid of me.

2) FEAR OF OTHERS

Most of the people you serve will love and appreciate you and will encourage you as they are able, but not all of them. Some will love you and have a wonderful plan for your life! Some will assign themselves to be the critics of your preaching and/or leadership. Some will be loyal and supportive, and some will do things that undermine your pastoral leadership. Some will give themselves to the ministry in sacrificial acts of service, and some will complain about the way they are being served. Some will approach you with loving candor, and some will give way to the temptation to talk behind your back. Some will jump in and get involved, while others will always relate to the church with a consumer's mentality. Some you will connect with easily, and with others you will find relationships much more difficult.

Because your ministry will always be done with people and for people, it is vital that people are in the right place in your heart. You cannot allow fear of people to close you off to others' perspectives or make you unwilling to delegate ministry tasks, nor can you allow fear to let others set the agenda so that they wrongly control the direction of the ministry to which God has called you. You cannot allow yourself to minister with a closed door, and you cannot be so sensitive to the opinions of others that you are unable to lead.

Because all the people you minister with and to are still dealing with indwelling sin, relationships and ministry with them will be messy. People will hurt you and damage your ministry. People will demand of you what they should not demand and will respond to you in ways they should not respond. In the middle of all of this, particular people, those who are influential and vocal, will loom larger than they should in your thoughts and motives. They will be afforded more power to influence you and the way you do ministry than they should. Rather than working for the glory of God, you will be tempted to work for their approval. Or, rather than working for the glory of God, you will work to disarm or expose them. In both cases your ministry is being corrupted by an ancient human fear—the fear of man.

The power that fear of man has to divert or delude ministry is powerfully portrayed in Galatians 2:11–14. Peter not only compromised, but he forsook the ministry to the Gentiles to which God had called him (see Acts 10) because he was afraid of "the circumcision party." Paul's critique was that Peter's conduct "was not in step with the truth of the gospel," so he confronted Peter. How much ministry is diverted by actions, reactions, and responses that are rooted not in fear of God but in fear of man? How often does this compromise the work of the gospel? How often does this cause people to stumble? How often are we tempted to act in a way that does not accord with what we say we believe? How much is fear of man setting the agenda in our churches? With openness and humility we need to keep asking these questions.

I wish I could say I am free of this fear, but I'm not. What about you? There have been times when I've found myself thinking, as I was preparing a sermon, that a particular point would finally win over one of my detractors. In that moment my preaching was about to be shaped not by my zeal for God's glory but by my hope that what I said would cause someone to finally see my glory. I understand that this is an ongoing war for the rule of my heart for which I have been given powerful, ever-present grace.

3) FEAR OF CIRCUMSTANCES

Since you don't author your own story, and since you haven't penned the script of your own ministry, there is a constant unpredictability to life and ministry. In this world of the unexpected, you are always living in the tension between who God is and what he's promised and the unexpected things that are on your plate. In the intersection between promise and reality, you have to be very careful to guard your meditation. You have to be very disciplined when it comes to what you do with your mind. Permit me to explain.

Abraham had been told by God that his descendants would be like the sand on the seashore, and he had staked his life on this promise. Now, the normal expectation would be that his wife, Sarah, would give birth early and often. But that did not happen. All throughout Sarah's childbearing years she was unable to conceive. Now both she and Abraham were old, way too old to seriously think that they would be blessed with the promised son. Old Abraham was now living in the tension between God's promise and the facts of his circumstance. When you're in the intersection between the promises of God and the details of your situation, what you do with your mind is very important. In this intersection, God will never ask you to deny reality. Abraham did not deny reality. Romans 4 says that he "considered the barrenness of Sarah's womb" (v. 19). Faith doesn't deny reality. No, it is a God-focused way of considering reality.

But the passage tells you more. It tells you what Abraham did with his meditation. He didn't invest himself in turning his circumstances inside out and over and over. No, he considered his circumstances, but he meditated on God. And as he meditated on God, he actually grew stronger in faith even though nothing in his circumstances had changed yet. For many people in ministry, waiting becomes a chronicle of ever-weakening faith because meditating on the circumstances will leave you in awe of the circumstances. They will appear to grow larger, you will feel smaller, and your vision of God will be clouded. But if you meditate on the Lord, you will be in greater awe of his presence, power, faithfulness, and grace. The situation will seem smaller, and you will live with greater confidence even though nothing has changed. Have the circumstances captured your meditation? Are there ways in which you have grown weaker in faith? Or do the eyes of your heart focus on a God who is infinitely greater than anything you will ever face?

4) FEAR OF THE FUTURE

You always live and minister in the hardship of not knowing. In both life and ministry you are called to trust and obey and believe that God will guide and provide. You and I do not know what the next moment will bring, let alone the next month or year. Security is never to be found in our attempt to figure it all out or in trying to divine the secret will of God. His secret will is called his "secret will" because it is secret! Yet in all of this, because you are a rational human being, there is a desire to know, to figure it out ahead of time. The more you concentrate on the future, the more you'll give way to fear of the future, and the more you'll be confused and de-motivated in the here and now.

Not knowing is hard. It would be nice to know if that elder is going to succumb to the temptation of being divisive. It would be nice to know if the finances of the church are going to rebound. It would be nice to know how that new preaching series will be received, if those young missionaries will make all the adjustments that they need to make, or if you'll get the permits to build that needed worship space. The fact of the matter is that we find questions of the future hard to deal with because we find it difficult to trust God. The One that we have said we've put our trust in knows everything about the future because he controls every aspect of it. Our fear of the future exposes the struggle we have to trust him and, in trusting him, to rest in his guidance and care, even though we don't really know what is coming next. Awe of God really is the only way to be free of fear of what is coming next. When my trust in God is greater than my fear of the unknown, I will be able to rest, even though I don't have a clue what will greet me around the corner. Pastor, do you load the future on your shoulders, with all of its questions and concerns? Or do you give yourself to the work of the present, leaving what is to come in God's capable hands? How much are you haunted by the "what ifs"? Do you greet the unknown with expectancy or dread? Do God's presence and promises quiet your unanswerable questions about the future?

▲ ▲ ▲

SO, *WHERE DO WE GO FROM HERE?*

Fear is a daily battle that everyone in ministry is called to fight. Because we all tend at points to suffer from God amnesia, because we live in a fallen world, and because we do not write our own stories, being ruled by fear is always a clear and present danger. There are moments when all of us get captured. There are ways in which all of us get sidetracked. There are times when worry is a more powerful shaper of ministry than faith. There are times that dread is more powerful than trust. There are times when all of us are overwhelmed by our weaknesses or weighed down by the circumstances. There are times when fear causes all of us to be way too controlling. There are times that fear silences us when we need to speak and causes us to speak when we should be silent. There are times when fear causes all of us to do things we should not do or keeps us from doing what we have been called to do. So it is vital to ask, What in the world should we do about fear? Let me suggest four things.

1) HUMBLY OWN YOUR FEARS.

Fear is never defeated by denying its existence. I know it's hard for those called to be people of faith and to lead others into the faith to have to admit that they do things as a direct result of unfaith. Own your fear and run to the only One who is able to defeat it. Confess that you don't always remember his presence and his glory. Confess those places where you assess situations as if he didn't exist. Own the fact that you often love your comfort more than you love his glory. Confess that there are moments when you are more in awe of people than you are of him. And as you confess, rest in the surety of his acceptance, forgiveness, empowerment, and deliverance. His grace guarantees a day when fear will be no more.

2) CONFESS THOSE PLACES WHERE FEAR HAS PRODUCED BAD DECISIONS AND WRONG RESPONSES.

Admit to those places of duplicity, favoritism, and compromise that resulted from letting horizontal fear replace vertical awe. Confess the places where you have not lived with courage the gospel that you say you believe. Confess to the people whom, in fear, you sinned against by silence, gossip, control, disloyalty, idolatry, etc. And ask God to give you eyes to see the places where you are susceptible to fear and need to grow in faith.

3) PAY ATTENTION TO YOUR MEDITATION.

In local church ministry there are so many difficult burdens that could capture your mind. There are so many things you could worry about. There are so many messy relationships, unfinished conversations, unrepentant sins, unfinished agendas, and unknown conclusions. In ministry, in intensely practical ways you are always living between the already and the not yet. So it is vital to always be aware of what is capturing your meditation. What grabs your thoughts when you're driving or when you have a few quiet moments? Do you live Abraham's paradigm, not denying the existence of trouble but prohibiting trouble from dominating and controlling your meditation? Does God loom so large in your thoughts that you grow strong in faith, even in the middle of what is unexpected and difficult?

4) PREACH THE GOSPEL TO YOURSELF.

Because there will be many times when no one knows what you are thinking and therefore cannot interrupt your private conversation, you need to be committed to preaching the gospel to yourself. You need to preach a gospel that finds its hope not in your understanding and ability but in a God who is grand and glorious in every way and who has invaded your life and ministry by his grace. You need to preach a gospel to yourself that does not find its rest in you getting it right but in the righteousness of Jesus Christ. You need to preach a gospel to yourself that does not get its motivation from human success, respect, and acclaim but from plenteous grace, which you could never have earned. You need to tell yourself again and again that there is no pit of life or ministry so deep that Jesus isn't deeper. You need to call yourself to rest and faith when no one else knows that private sermon is needed.

▲ ▲ ▲

May grace cause you to have a ministry that is shaped by living faith and not by the long catalog of fears that greet each of us this side of our final home.

CHAPTER TEN

MEDIOCRITY

He rushed out at the end of the post-conference luncheon meeting with the staff of his church. It was about 2:30 p.m., and he was in a rush to get going because his sermon for the next day was hanging over his head. He told me he had some errands to do, which would be followed by dinner with his family, and then sometime in the evening he would lock himself in his home office and try to put together his message for the next day. No matter what happened the rest of that day, no matter how much time he was actually able to devote to his sermon, and no matter how well his preparation went, no matter how prepared he felt to deal with the text before him, he would get up the next day and say something.

I wondered how many pastors are in the same place and have developed the same ministry habits. I wondered how many throw something together at the last minute and how many sermons are not given the time necessary to communicate what needs to be communicated. I wondered how many congregations around the world are, plainly and simply, being poorly fed by unprepared pastors. I wondered how many sermons end up being boring restatements of favorite commentaries or little more than impersonal, poorly delivered theological lectures.

I don't need to wonder anymore. Having spoken at literally hundreds of churches around the world, I have experienced this Saturday afternoon sermon scenario over and over again. It has left me both sad and angry. No wonder people lack excitement with the gospel. No wonder they don't approach Sunday morning with anticipation. No wonder they quit believing that the Bible speaks to the drama of their everyday struggle. No wonder they quit thinking that their pastor can relate to what their life is like or to the questions that tend to haunt them. No wonder so many people in so many pews sit there with minds wandering and hearts disengaged. No wonder they find it hard to push the last week's problems or the next day's duties out of their minds as they sit there on Sunday morning.

I am very concerned about the acceptance of Sunday morning mediocrity, and I am persuaded that it is not primarily a schedule or laziness problem. I am convinced it is a theological problem. You see, the standards you set for yourself and your ministry are directly related to your view of God. If you are feeding your soul every day on the grace and glory of God, if you are in worshipful awe of his wisdom and power, if you are spiritually stunned by his faithfulness and love, and if you are daily motivated by his presence and promises, then you want to do everything you can to capture and display that glory to the people God has placed in your care. It is your job as a pastor to pass this glory down to another generation, and it is impossible for you to do that if you are not being awestricken by God's glory yourself.

Now, the stakes are high here. You could argue that every worship service is little more than a glory war. The great question of the gathering is, will the hearts of this group of people be captured by the one glory that is truly glorious or by the shadow glories of the created world? As a pastor, I want to do everything I can to be used of God to capture the hearts of those gathered by the rescuing glory of God's grace, by the insight-giving glory of God's wisdom, by the hope-giving glory of his love, by the empowering glory of his presence, by the rest-giving glory of his sovereignty, and by the saving glory of his Son. But I know that this is a battle. I am speaking to people whose hearts are fickle and easily distracted. I know I am talking to people who are seduced by other glories. I know I am talking to people who live in the light of God's glory every day and yet are capable of being functionally blind to its splendor.

I know I am addressing the single lady who has set her heart on the affection of a certain young man whom she thinks will deliver to her the happiness she has been craving. Sitting before me is the teenager who can't think beyond the glories of Facebook, Twitter, and the *Portal2* video game. In the congregation is the middle-aged man whose heart is captured by the glory of somehow, someway recapturing his youth. A wife is sitting there wondering if she will ever experience the glory of the kind of marriage that she dreamed about, the kind she knows others have. A man sits in the crowd knowing that he feeds his soul almost daily on the dark and distorted glories of pornography and has become a master at shifting spiritual gears. Some listening are more excited about a new outfit, new home, new car, new shotgun, newly sodded lawn, the opening of a new restaurant, a new vacation site, or that new promotion than they are about the good news of the gospel of Jesus Christ.

Of those who have gathered for worship, there are those distracted by grief, anger, discouragement, loneliness, envy, frustration, despair, or hopelessness, because the glories that they have looked to for their meaning, purpose, and inner happiness have failed them once again. These glories have proven to be more temporary than they thought they would ever be. They have been more elusive than they seemed at a distance. They have blown up in their faces or dripped like sand through their fingers. And even when they were wonderful to experience, they didn't, in fact, leave their hearts satisfied. The buzz was short and the satisfaction elusive. So they sit there empty, hurt, angry, and confused.

They come into worship in the middle of a war that they probably don't recognize. It is a war for the allegiance, the worship, of their hearts. In ways they probably don't understand, they have again and again asked the creation to give them what only the Creator can provide. They have looked horizontally again and again for what can only be found vertically. They have asked people, situations, locations, and experiences to be the one thing they will never be: their savior. They have looked to these things to give them life, security, identity, and hope. They have asked these things to heal their broken hearts. They have hoped that these things would make them better people. So a war rages, and wounded soldiers sit before you. It is a glory war, a battle for what glory will rule their hearts and, in so doing, control their choices, words, and behaviors.

Along with this there really is an enemy who will do anything he can with lies, seduction, distraction, and deceit to keep my heart from focusing on the glory for which I was created to live, the glory of God. So it is a high and holy calling to step into the middle of this glory war commissioned to be one of God's primary tools to recapture the wandering hearts of battle-scarred and battle-weary soldiers.

For others, following this God of glory has seemed to be anything but glorious. They were expecting joy and blessing, and what they got is pain, sadness, and trial. They find it increasingly hard to believe those glorious truths that God is near, that he hears, that he cares, that he is faithful, that he is wise, that he exercises his power for the good of his children, and that he is loving, kind, gracious, and patient. They feel that they've been forsaken. They feel they're being punished. They are being tempted to conclude that what they were taught was true isn't really true after all. They wonder why they have been singled out for suffering that others don't seem to be going through. They wonder why they pray and nothing seems to happen. They have quit reading their Bible because it doesn't seem to help, and they find that the songs on Sunday morning seem to be describing a very different reality from the one they live in. They've quit asking for prayer for the same things over and over again in their small group because it just makes them feel like a loser. They feel that the glory that was put before them has eluded them completely, and they don't know what to do about it. So, without being conscious of it, they have begun to offer their hearts to other glories, hoping that somehow, someway, satisfaction will be found.

Pastor, to these beaten-down ones you have been called as an ambassador of glory. You have been called to rescue those who are awe discouraged and awe confused. You are called to represent the One who is glory, to people who, by means of suffering and disappointment, have become glory cynics. You have been called to be God's voice to woo them back. You are placed in their lives as a divine means of rescue, healing, and restoration. You have been called to speak into the confusion with gospel clarity and authority. You have been called to give glory-bound hope to those who have become hopeless. You are called to speak liberating truths to those who have become deceived. You have been called to plead with disloyal children to once again be reconciled to their heavenly Father. You have been called to give glorious motivation to those who have given up. You have been called to shine the light of the glory of God into hearts that have been made dark by looking for life in all the wrong places. You have been called to offer the filling glories of grace to those who are empty and malnourished. You have been called to represent a glorious King, who alone is able to rescue, heal, redeem, transform, forgive, deliver, and satisfy. You have been called.

GOD'S GLORY, OUR EXCELLENCE

If your heart is in functional awe of the glory of God, then there will be no place in your heart for poorly prepared, badly delivered, functional pastoral mediocrity. Permit me to explain. I think we should all be shocked at the level of mediocrity that we tolerate in the life and ministry of the local church. No, I'm not talking about giving people room to grow and mature and not crushing them with criticism in the process. I'm talking about those places where our standards are simply too low, places where we could and should do much, much better. And I am convinced that if awe of God doesn't reign in our hearts, then that awe won't shape our preparation for and delivery of the things that God has called us to do in ministry.

Mediocrity is not a time, personnel, resource, or location problem. Mediocrity is a heart problem. We have lost our commitment to the highest levels of excellence because we have lost our awe. Awe amnesia is the open door that admits mediocrity. Awe of God is fear-producing, inspiring, motivating, convicting, and commitment-producing. There is no replacement for this in the leadership of the church of Jesus Christ. Awe protects us from us by asking more of us than we would ever ask of ourselves. Awe reminds us that it is not about us and so keeps us from dropping our guard when it might be convenient to do so.

Awe reminds you that God is so glorious that it is impossible for you, as his ambassador, to have ministry standards that are too high. I'm not talking about lavish, expensively furnished buildings. No, I'm talking about a sturdy commitment to do everything you can to display the glory of his presence and grace as powerfully and clearly as you can each time his people are gathered. You are in such awe of, and have been so satisfied by, his grace yourself that you have a zeal to display that grace to those under your care, a zeal you can get no other way. You are never just doing your duty. You are never just cranking it out. You are never just going through the motions. You are never just putting on a front. You are worshiping your way through whatever you are doing at that moment as the ambassador of an expansively glorious King. And you are in reverential fear of doing anything that would dent, diminish, or desecrate that glory in any way. As a pastor, you are a glory-captured tool for the capture of others.

It is here again that we are faced with the fact that our ministries are not shaped just by knowledge, experience, and skill but by the true condition of our hearts. Excellence in ministry flows from a heart that is in holy, reverential, life-rearranging, motivation-capturing awe of the Lord of glory. In fact, it is even deeper than that. Excellence is, in fact, a relationship. There is only one who is truly and perfectly excellent. He alone is the sum and definition of what excellence is and does. So the One who is excellence, in his grace, came to you when you were in a state of anything but excellence and, by grace, offered you the promise of actually becoming a partaker of his divine nature. He then connects you to purposes and goals way higher, way grander and more glorious, than you would ever have sought for yourself. By grace he causes you to think what you wouldn't have thought and to desire what you had never before wanted. He opens your eyes to his glory. He opens the door to his kingdom. Your hope of ever being excellent in his eyes and doing what is excellent in his sight is found in your relationship to him and in his grace that not only forgives and accepts but radically transforms. And he calls and empowers you to display his excellency and the excellency of his grace. It is only this excellency that has the power to free us from the false excellency of human pride and the mediocrity that results when we are okay with ourselves and our world just the way they are.

It is when I am in awe at the reality that I have, by grace alone, been attached to what is truly excellent in every way that I want to be an ambassador of that excellence. I want others to experience the excellent grace that is freeing me from me and can free them as well. When this is true, I become committed to displaying the glory of that excellence in every way that is possible in the scope of my ministry. This means I will be sobered as I consider my calling to be the ambassador of the God of such glory, and I will be in awe of being called to put his grace on display. So I will have high standards for every aspect of the ministry that is under my care. Whether it is children's or youths' ministries, men's or women's ministries, small groups or outreach, whether it is leadership training or short-term missions, public worship or preaching, I will want each ministry of the church to be done in excellence so that they will faithfully display the excellence of the One who calls out of darkness into his marvelous light.

This means we will be committed to the disciplines that cause these ministries to be as free from chaos and mediocrity as is possible between the already and the not yet. First, we must be committed to preaching the gospel to ourselves, reminding ourselves of our ongoing need to be rescued from us and the low standards to which sin attracts us. We constantly remind ourselves of how we are tempted to value what is expedient and comfortable rather than what is excellent in the eyes of God. And we tell ourselves again and again that for these battles we have been given bountiful, right-here, right-now grace.

This also means that we will do everything to maintain relationships of unity, understanding, and love between us. We know we are sinners. We know we will sin against one another. We know there are moments when we will be disappointed and hurt. We know we will be misunderstood and wrongly judged. We know we will be selfish and controlling, self-righteous and demanding. We know we will ask one another to give what we have already been given in Christ. So we determine to give ourselves the humility of approachability and the courage of loving honesty. We will commit ourselves to regular patterns of confession and forgiveness. And we will celebrate together the grace that enables sinners to live and minister alongside sinners in a community of unity and love.

And we will be committed to the discipline of adequate preparation that enables us to do well what we have been called to do. You cannot have a ministry that is committed to ambassadorial excellence if these things (disciplines) are not a regular part of your community. If you forget who you are, your ministry will be shaped by a smugness that is more about displaying how great you are than about how glorious the Savior is, the Savior who is still meeting you in your weakness. If you are not committed to loving gospel community, you will minister out of frustration and discouragement, displaying God's glory in an abstract form but not in its living, life-changing vitality. And if you are not committed to the discipline of preparation, you will offer sloppy leadership to poorly sighted people that will become more of a distraction from, rather than an enhancement of, their ability to see God for who is he and place their hope in him.

PREACHING AND THE GOD WHO IS EXCELLENT

I want to examine one place where I think there is entirely too much mediocrity in the church of Jesus Christ—preaching. I want to talk about preaching. Because of what God has called me to do, I get to be in churches around the world. For about forty weekends each year, I am with some body of Christ somewhere in the world. Often I am not able to return home on Saturday, so I will attend the service of the local congregation (when I am not scheduled to preach). What I am about to say will probably get me into trouble, but I am convinced it needs to be said. I am saddened and distressed to say it, but I am tired of hearing boring, inadequately prepared theological lectures read as manuscripts that will inspire no one by uninspired preachers—all done in the name of biblical preaching. There is a way in which, if you examine the whole process, it is neither biblical nor preaching! I am not surprised in these moments that people's minds wander. I am not surprised that people are struggling to keep attentive and awake. I am surprised that more aren't. They are being taught by one who has not brought the proper weapons into the pulpit to fight for them and with them the spiritual war that every moment of preaching actually is.

Preaching is more than the regurgitation of your favorite exegetical commentary, or a rather transparent recast of the sermons of your favorite preachers, or a reshaping of notes from one of your favorite seminary classes. It is bringing the transforming truths of the gospel of Jesus Christ from a passage that has been properly understood, cogently and practically applied, and delivered with the engaging tenderness and passion of a person who has been broken and restored by the very truths he stands up to communicate. You simply cannot do this without proper preparation, meditation, confession, and worship.

There simply is no way that you can begin to think about a passage for the first time on Saturday afternoon or evening and give it the kind of attention that it needs so that you understand and have been personally impacted by it and are prepared to give it to others in a way that is understandable and consumable and contributes to their ongoing transformation. As pastors, we have to fight for the sanctity of preaching, or no one else will. We have to demand that we are afforded the time in our job descriptions that is necessary to prepare well. We have to carve out time in our schedules to do whatever is necessary for each of us, given our gifts and maturity, to be ready to be a spokesman for our Savior king. We cannot become comfortable with patterns that denigrate preaching and degrade our ability to represent well a glorious God of glorious grace. We cannot allow ourselves to be too busy and too distracted. We cannot set low standards for ourselves and those we serve. We cannot be self-excusing and self-accommodating. We cannot allow ourselves to try to squeeze a thousand dollars' worth of preparation into dime moments. We must determine to do everything we can to enter each moment of preaching well prepared. We must not lose sight of the excellent One and the excellent grace we have been called to represent. We cannot, because we are unprepared, let his splendor appear boring and his amazing grace appear run-of-the-mill.

The culture and discipline that surround our preaching always reveal the true character of our own hearts. This is exactly where confession and repentance need to take place. We cannot allow ourselves to blame our job descriptions or our busyness. We cannot allow ourselves to point the finger at the unexpected things that show up on the schedule of every pastor. We cannot allow ourselves to blame the demands of family. We have to humbly confess that our preaching is mediocre, not rising to the standard to which we have been called, and then that the problem is us. The problem is that we have lost our awe, and in losing our awe we are all too comfortable with representing God's excellence in a way that is anything but excellent. Ministry mediocrity in any form is always an issue of the heart. If this describes you, then run in humble confession to your Savior and embrace the grace that has the power to rescue you from you and, in so doing, to give you back your awe.

It is important to understand the two essential parts of effective preaching and how each requires its own discipline of preparation. First, there is the *content* part of preaching. Preaching is all about accurately exegeting and understanding the truths of the gospel as they are unfolded in a particular passage of Scripture. I cannot rush this aspect of my preparation. I cannot leave the discipline of content until I have understood the purpose for and gospel content of the passage before me. And I must understand that if I am unable to practically apply the truths of the passage to my life and to those to whom I will preach, then I haven't yet fully understood the passage. The exegetical process doesn't end with understanding; it ends with application. Preaching is not just about "this is what this means"; it is also about "this is what it means to live in light of what this means."

It is my experience that exegesis that ends with the pastor's ability to apply what he has learned from the passage before him isn't an event, but a process. It is necessary for me to live with a passage, to carry it around with me and to marinate my soul with its nourishing and thirst-quenching waters. I simply can't do this in a couple hours. I need meditative time with the passage so that the Spirit can work through it in me and through me to the people under my ministry. I'm about to make some of you mad, but I'm going to say it. If you are developing original content late on a Saturday evening, you have no business preaching it on Sunday. It's unlikely that you will have understood the full range of the radical gospel glories of the passage, it's doubtful that they have had any time whatsoever to confront your own heart, and it's unlikely that you have developed much readiness to communicate them winsomely and practically to your listeners.

At that late hour you will settle for a surface scan of the passage and call it a sermon; you will pirate the work of others even if you don't know you're doing it, and you will have little ability to portray well the radical confrontation and encouragement of the gospel of Jesus Christ. Because you have not taken the time necessary, you will preach theological stuff, depersonalized doctrinal bits and pieces that are disassociated from the gospel of grace. You will communicate ideas, but you will not powerfully preach a glorious Christ, who is powerfully present in every passage you will ever be called to preach. You will default to offering people a system of redemption (theology and rules), but you will not help them to find their hope and help in a redeemer. So your people will think they're growing in maturity because they are growing in theological understanding, but your preaching will not bring them to the end of themselves and to the cross of Jesus Christ. We must always, always, remember that the theology of the Word of God is not an end in itself but a means to an end, and that end is a radically grace-transformed life.

But there is a second essential aspect to preaching. Preaching is not just a craft of content; it is also a craft of *communication*. You must meditate, pray, labor, wrestle, and work on how to communicate the truths that you have come to understand to the particular people who are in your care. I am persuaded that we have devalued the communication aspect of powerful, effective, life-changing gospel preaching. I am not talking about your trying to be a John Piper or a Tim Keller. No, I'm talking about your commitment to do everything you can to winsomely and cogently explain and apply the glorious truths that you exegeted as you undertook the necessary discipline of content. You have no time whatsoever to develop the communication aspect of your sermon—to think of a helpful turn of phrase, an illuminating personal illustration, or a practical point of gospel application—if the process hasn't begun until Saturday. You're just relieved that you got the content down, that you actually have something to say when it comes time to stand up and preach. But you won't say things well, you won't develop insight-giving word pictures, you won't have that tender moment of self-disclosing honesty, you won't make specific application to the culture that your people live in, you won't show your people that every truth revealed in the passage is a finger that points to Christ, and you won't leave people hungering for more. You have entered the pulpit with a bag of content, but it hasn't yet been formed into a sermon.

I think of the relationship between these two aspects of preaching much the way I think about cooking. I love to cook, so I am the one in our family who cooks the Thanksgiving and Christmas feasts. Now, if you have purposed to feed your family a wonderful, memorable meal, it all starts with gathering fine ingredients. If you don't take the time to hunt for the best ingredients available, you will never have that good meal of your dreams. The gathering of the best ingredients is analogous to the *content* part of preaching. Good preaching is rooted in the gathering of fine gospel ingredients out of the passage before you. But on Thanksgiving Day, I don't put ingredients on the table. Ingredients are the substance of a meal, but they are not a meal. They must be formed into attractive, tasty, nutritious, and consumable elements that together form a meal. A hunk of butter and a mouthful of flour followed by a spoon of cornmeal is not very appetizing or digestible, but cornbread is a wonderful thing. The finest of turkeys placed raw on a table would be neither appealing nor edible. The forming of the fine ingredients collected into a beautiful meal is analogous to the *communication* aspect of preaching.

I am afraid that many preachers out there are in the sad habit of putting ingredients on the table. They may be fine ingredients, but, regrettably, they have not been formed into a meal, so they are neither attractive nor consumable. If everyone I feed were a chef, I would be able to put ingredients on the table so that they could form it into a meal; but they aren't. And if everyone to whom you are preaching were a preacher/pastor, you could put gospel ingredients on the table so they could form them into a meal; but they are not. No, I am not discounting the Holy Spirit's power to capture, convict, and change people through his Word. There is not a moment in preaching where we are not utterly dependent on him, and we are never called to do his work. But the Holy Spirit has commissioned us to be his instruments, and our job is to do everything we can to be sharp instruments in his redemptive hands.

I will tell you what this means for me. It means that I can't have a fresh encounter with the truths I am to communicate from a particular portion of Scripture on the week that they are to be preached. A week does not give me enough content and communication time. I work ahead to prepare to preach wherever I am called. This means that when I prepare the content of a message, it is the message that I'll be preaching in three or four weeks. This gives time for truths to marinate in my own heart and become more deeply and practically understood. On the week that the sermon is to be preached, I preach it aloud to myself some fifteen or twenty times. As I do this, both my understanding of the passage and the creative ways it can be communicated deepen and develop.

Now, I'm not suggesting that this regimen of preparation is the right one for you, but I am suggesting that we cannot be satisfied with poorly prepared exegetical meanderings delivered by a pastor who doesn't see his own mediocrity because his heart needs to be recaptured by the awe of God's glory and grace. God's presence in our preaching and his grace that meets us in our weakness assure us that we can do better.

Pastor, are you suffering from an awe amnesia that allows you to set standards way lower than required if you are going to take your ambassadorial calling seriously? Has awe amnesia allowed you to be comfortable with mediocrity in ministry, which is a functional contradiction of the glories you celebrate? If so, don't wallow in shame; don't hide in guilt. Run to your Redeemer. Bask in his glorious grace. Seek the forgiveness and empowerment that only he can give. And commit yourself, by his grace, to the disciplines of excellence that will only ever happen as he recues you from you and gives you back your awe once again.

CHAPTER ELEVEN

BETWEEN THE ALREADY AND THE NOT YET

I wasn't consciously proud. Maybe most proud people aren't conscious of how proud they really are. But I felt that I had arrived. In ways that now shock and embarrass me, I thought of myself as a grace graduate. I didn't minister out of my own need. I had done very well in seminary. I had planted a church in a very hard place. I had founded a Christian school that was growing rapidly. (Both the church and the school I had founded along with others, but I didn't look at it that way.) I was getting invitations all over the place to speak. In ways that are hard for me to imagine now, I thought I had spiritually arrived. I had a scary self-assurance. I often looked at the people I was ministering to with a self-congratulatory pity, assuming, of course, that they were essentially different from me. No, I didn't make fun of people, and I didn't spend my time bragging about my accomplishments, but an attitude of arrival did shape my ministry.

I was incredibly impatient and often quietly irritated. I found it hard to delegate ministry to others. I wanted more control than was actually necessary and productive. I gave my opinion way too often. I treated the ministries God had called me to as if they belonged to me. I wanted people to quickly sign on to support my brainstorms. My sermons were rather arrogant lectures—you know, the final word on the topic or the passage. I once preached what I thought was the ultimate sermon on pride that was actually a living example of the same! My preaching and teaching was more law than gospel. This is typical of a person who thinks he is a law keeper.

As a pastor, I was making a dangerous self-assessment mistake. I had bought into a fallacious, distorted view of my spiritual maturity. This view is both very tempting and very comfortable for people in ministry, and when we buy into this view, it sets us up for a catalog of temptations. Rather than looking at myself in the accurate mirror of the Word of God—the only place where you will get both an accurate definition of spiritual maturity and a reliable read on your own spiritual condition—I looked elsewhere. I looked to excellent grades and student prizes in seminary to tell me how mature I was. It is a dangerous intellectual and knowledge-based method of assessing your spiritual condition. I looked to ministry skill to tell me how spiritually mature I was, forgetting that God gives gifts to whomever he wills. I looked to my ministry experience; the years of labor made me feel spiritually seasoned and mature.

Rather than humbly standing before the honest assessment of the mirror of the Bible to see myself as I really was, I looked into carnival mirrors. Now, the problem with the carnival mirror is that it really does show you *you*, but with distortion. You don't actually have a 20-inch-high neck and a 6-inch torso; yes, it's you in that concave mirror, but it's not showing you the way you actually look. The danger of assessments of arrival greets everyone in ministry. The danger that you would quit thinking of yourself as weak and needy is always near. The danger that you would see yourself as being in a different category from those to whom you minister is right around the corner. This danger greets you every day because there are carnival mirrors all around that have the power to give you a distorted view of you. And when you think you've arrived, when you quit being convicted of and broken by your own weakness, failures, and sins, you will begin to make bad personal and ministry choices. The reality and confession of personal spiritual weakness is not a grave danger to your ministry. God has chosen to build his church through the instrumentality of bent and broken tools. It is your delusions of strength that will get you in trouble and cause you to form a ministry that is less than Christ-centered and gospel-driven.

When I hear a sermon that is essentially law-driven, that is, asking the law to do what only the grace of Jesus Christ can accomplish, I am immediately concerned about the preacher. I immediately wonder about his view of himself, because if he had any self-consciousness about his own weakness and sin, he would find little hope and comfort for himself and his hearers in that kind of sermon. You see this dynamic in the Pharisees. Because they thought of themselves as righteous, perfect law givers, they had no problem laying unbearable law burdens on others. Their misuse of the law had its roots not only in bad theology but also in ugly human pride. They saw law keeping as possible, because they thought they were keeping it. And they thought that others should get up and keep it as well as they did. They were the religious leaders of their day, but they were arrogant, insensitive, uncompassionate, and judgmental. They were not part of what God was doing at the moment; no, they were in the way of it.

I am afraid that there is a whole lot of pride in the modern pulpit. There is a whole lot of pride in the seminary classroom. There is a whole lot of pride in the church staff. It is one of the reasons for all the relational conflict that takes place in the church. It is why we are often better theological gatekeepers than tender and humble spokesmen for the gospel. It is why pastors often seem unapproachable. It is why we get angry in meetings or defensive when someone disagrees with us or points out a wrong. We are too self-assured. We are too confident. We too quickly assess that we are okay. We too quickly make heroes out of ourselves and others. We too often take credit for what sovereign grace produced. We too often assess that we don't need the help that the normal believer needs. We are too quick to speak and too slow to listen. We too often take as personal affronts things that are not personal. We quit being students too soon. We don't see ourselves as needy often enough. We have too little meditative-communion-with-Christ time nailed into our schedules. We confidently assign to ourselves more ministry work than we can do. We live in more isolation than is spiritually healthy. Pastor, there is ample evidence all around us that we tend to forget who we are and that we allow ourselves to be defined by things that should not define us.

Let me say again: if you are a pastor or ministry leader, you are at the same time a person in the middle of your own sanctification. You are not yet free of sin and all its attendant dangers. You still carry around moral susceptibility. You are capable of giving way to disastrous things. You are capable of losing your way. You are capable of ungodly attitudes and dark desires. You have not been completely delivered from pride, greed, lust, anger, and bitterness. There are places where you are an idolater, where the agenda is being set by a desire for some created thing more than it is by worship of your Creator. You do not always minister as an ambassador. There are times when you do your ministry work with the attitude of a king rather than as one called to represent the King. You do not always love God above all else. You do not always love your neighbor as yourself. You are not always kind and compassionate. You are not always patient and forgiving. There are moments when you love your little kingdom of one more than you love God's kingdom. There are times when you love comfort and pleasure more than you love redemption. There are times when pride renders you unkind and unapproachable. There are times when you want your ministry to be about you. There are times when you're irritated by the very people you've been called to pastor. You are not proud of all your thoughts. You would not want your congregation to hear all your words. You do things in private moments that you would not want seen in public.

These things are true of me as well. And they give evidence to the fact that we who are called to provide and lead ministry are in desperate need of ministry ourselves. We who proclaim the message of grace are deeply in need of grace ourselves. We have not arrived. We have not moved beyond a moment-by-moment need for grace. We are not yet out of danger. We are not yet free from temptation. The war for our hearts still rages. We still fall and fail. We simply have not arrived, but we are tempted to think we have because we buy into false assessments of our spiritual condition.

LOOKING INTO THE CARNIVAL MIRRORS OF MINISTRY

Because we are all tempted to be self-sufficient and to think that we are independently righteous, we are all attracted to overinflated, aggrandized views of ourselves. To use Paul's words, we think of ourselves "more highly than we ought to think" (see Rom. 12:3). We all tend to want to have our righteousness recognized and confirmed. We all want to be seen as right and mature. We all want to be looked up to and esteemed. So we are attracted to things that seem to define us as Christlike and mature. In a word, we all are susceptible to having our definition of ourselves formed by the carnival mirrors that are in every ministry person's life. Remember, no mirror that you look into to know yourself will ever show you *you* with the clarity and accuracy of the mirror of the Word of God. Let me suggest four of those mirrors.

1) THE MIRROR OF MINISTRY KNOWLEDGE

Biblical literacy and theological understanding are very important things; after all, God chose to make his greatest revelation of himself and his plan in a book. It is a book you must determine to know in every way. It's a book the truth themes of which you must grow to understand as thoroughly as possible. You must see the fabric of truth, that is, how truths are interwoven and connect to one another. You must understand the flow of the plan of redemption. Biblical knowledge is a vital, essential, and irreplaceable thing; but it must not be confused with true faith or personal spiritual maturity. Faith is deeply more than what you do with your brain. Knowledge is an aspect of faith, but it doesn't define faith. Ultimately, faith is an investment of the heart that leads to a radically new way of living your life. Spiritual maturity is more than maturity of knowledge. You can actually be mature in your understanding of God's sovereignty but live a life of fear, because in your immaturity you have attached your security more to your control than to God's wise rule. It is not an oxymoron to say that there are loads of theologically knowledgeable pastors who, in the way that they live and minister, are spiritually immature. Your level of biblical, theological knowledge is not a safe mirror into which to look to assess your spiritual maturity.

2) THE MIRROR OF MINISTRY EXPERIENCE

The longer you've been in ministry, the more ministry blocks you've been around, and the more ministry knocks you've taken, the more it feels like you've arrived. You're no longer wet behind your ministry ears. You're no longer new to the push and pull of local church ministry. You probably won't be surprised by what will happen next because you've just about seen it all. You have come to know that ministry is war. You know that it is often as disappointing as it is exciting. You know that you'll have both your detractors and your celebrants. You know the pressures you will face, balancing ministry and family. You know that local-church ministry is seasonal. No, I'm not talking about the weather here. I mean that pastors tend to go through good and bad seasons of ministry. So all of this experience makes you feel that you're mature; but it can be a dangerous and distorted mirror to look into.

The fact is that there is a critical difference between the street-level wisdom gained from experience and spiritual maturity. You can know what is going to happen next, because you've been around the block a few times, but you may not deal well with what is going to happen next, because you lack maturity. If all that was needed to form maturity was a certain amount of experience, not only would there be many more mature people, but Jesus would not have had to come. Experience will teach you some things, but it simply has no power to make you holy. Sadly, when you let experience tell you that you are mature when you're not, you quit being committed to change because you don't think it's needed.

3) THE MIRROR OF MINISTRY SUCCESS

It is very tempting to try to get your identity from your ministry success. But local-church ministry success is the result of things that are profoundly deeper than a leader's insights, strategic planning, sense of the moments, ability to build a ministry team, and instilling a compelling ministry vision in the congregation. If our human ministry efforts are not propelled by God's powerful grace and applied by the Holy Spirit, they will be for nothing. It is Christ and Christ alone who builds his church. This is humbling stuff because it requires us to admit that we have no power whatsoever to change anyone. We have no ability to advance God's kingdom. So ministry success always says more about the Lord we serve than it does about us. Ministry success is not a valid measuring instrument of our maturity. In fact, a God of grace will bless our ministries in spite of us because of his zeal for his church and his commitment to his own glory.

4) THE MIRROR OF MINISTRY CELEBRITY

Pastoral-ministry celebrity is simply a dangerous thing. The people who are exposed only to your public ministry persona, your books or Internet blogs, and your voice when it is in a conference or on a DVD are functionally incapable of giving you an accurate view of yourself. You must take their congratulatory words as well meant but lacking in accuracy and, therefore, spiritual helpfulness. They haven't seen you in your private domain, they do not know your heart, and they have not interviewed those who live nearest to you. Having said all this, it is still tempting to listen too much to your own press. It is tempting to think you have arrived because people treat you as if you're something special. It is tempting to forget who you really are. Public acclaim is often the seedbed for spiritual pride. The question of pastoral maturity cannot be answered by people who appreciate you but, frankly, don't really know you at all.

▲ ▲ ▲

Pastor, do you examine yourself daily by humbly placing yourself before the one mirror you can trust, the mirror of the Word of God? Or have you fallen into the habit of looking into carnival mirrors that will only ever give you a misshapen view of where you are in your personal spiritual journey?

THE DANGEROUS RESULTS OF THINKING YOU'VE ARRIVED

I didn't see it at the time, but I enjoyed the ministry celebrity that I experienced during my early days in coal country. I was the center of a little growing church and a rapidly growing Christian school, and I loved it. We were seeing fruit in a place where there hadn't been much fruit, and people were excited. Thankful people seemed to be everywhere, and they expressed their thanks often. But, in ways I didn't see then, I took a lot of the credit. I was unaware of how proud I had become until a man asked if he could meet with me. I was sure he had been convicted by one of my glorious sermons and wished to counsel with me. We met over dinner, a meal that neither one of us ended up eating, and it quickly became clear that he didn't want to talk about himself; he wanted to talk about me. He spent a couple hours giving me example after example of my pride. He said that he thought that I thought my job was to give "the final opinion on everything."

I was devastated. I thought he had been inaccurate and unkind. But I couldn't escape his words, so I called my brother Tedd to ask him what I should do. Tedd gave me the best and hardest advice. He simply said, "Listen." Over the next few weeks I tried my best to stop, look, and listen, and what I saw was a proud man who had begun in subtle and not so subtle ways to take credit for what only grace could produce. I heard a man speaking who had forgotten who he was. I saw a young pastor who had already begun to act as if he had arrived. I wish I could say that I am free of all the self-assessment delusions of my ministry youth, but I am not. There are times when the congratulatory comments of a thankful hearer will morph into self-congratulation. At times I am defensive when someone presumes to question or confront me. There are times when I am too self-aware and not nearly as Christ-aware as I should be. You see, I still struggle because there is still latent self-righteousness in me, and the praise of others tends to confirm the praise for myself that I still carry around in my heart. So I still cry out for help. I still need to be rescued from me. I still have but one hope: the transforming grace of Jesus Christ.

So what are the lifestyle tendencies of a pastor who is living and ministering from a position of arrival? Well, if you think you've arrived:

1) YOU WILL THINK THAT YOU DON'T NEED WHAT YOU PREACH.
Sinclair Ferguson said in a post-conference question-and-answer session that he had determined to be a man who sat under his own

preaching. Even your preparation should be an acknowledgment of ongoing need, a cry for divine help, and a celebration of ever-present, inexhaustible grace. This is the "I am a man of unclean lips and I dwell amongst people of unclean lips" of Isaiah 6:5. If you think you have arrived, you prepare material from above for people who sadly still need what you no longer need. Are you desperately hungry for the truths that you regularly prepare to expound to others?

2) YOU WILL NOT BE OPEN TO THE MINISTRY OF THE BODY OF CHRIST.

Arrival tends to produce self-sufficiency. If you think you're wise, you don't seek out the wisdom of others. If you think you're mature, you don't hunger for the protection of others. If you see yourself as a person of mature faith, you don't seek the courage-giving encouragement of others. If you don't see your sin, you won't see the value of confessing it to those who can counsel and warn you. If you think you're up to whatever temptation will be thrown at you, you don't ask for other eyes to watch out for you and other hearts to pray on your behalf. Arrival, whether conscious or not, will always begin to cut you off from the essential protecting and sanctifying ministry of the body of Christ.

3) YOU WILL EXPECT OF OTHERS THE PERFECTION THAT YOU THINK YOU'VE ACHIEVED.

Arrival is not the soil in which pastoral grace grows. People who think of themselves as righteous tend to expect and require of others the same righteousness that they think they have achieved. Rather than being the soil in which grace grows, arrival is the soil in which unrealistic expectation, criticism, impatience, and harsh judgments grow. I can't tell you how many staff members have shared with me that their relationship to their senior pastor (and these are my words) is characterized more by law than by grace. If you think you are keeping the law, then you are comfortable with throwing the law at others. But if you are grieved at the reality that you daily fall woefully short of God's requirement, that your rest is not in your own righteousness but in the righteousness of Christ, then you will naturally minister to others the same grace that you so desperately need and so graciously receive from God's hand.

4) YOU WILL FEEL QUALIFIED TO HAVE MORE CONTROL THAN YOU HAVE.

If you come to be impressed by your own wisdom and strength, if you mount up evidence for your own righteousness, then it makes sense that you would be self-assured, thinking that you're more capable, more ready to deal with whatever God puts on your plate, than you actually are. Because you are convinced that you are strong and wise, it is natural to assess that you should be in control. You don't carry around in you the hunger for wisdom you don't have or for protection from personal weaknesses. You aren't concerned that your control could be tainted by sin, that is, that it could degrade into control for self-interest and self-aggrandizement.

Let's be honest. There are too many power struggles in the local church. Gospel ministry easily becomes politicized. Pride causes you to hunger for power (even though you may not know it); the hunger for power causes you to collect ministry allies, and the desire for control causes you to locate ministry enemies. Somehow, someway, gospel ministry has become a political battleground for human power. This is a form of ministry that has lost its center. Jesus has left the building. A king is being put forward, but not *the* King. A kingdom is being built, but not *the* kingdom. If as a pastor you are being pastoral, you are doing it for others, but if as a pastor you have gone political, you are doing it for you.

5) YOU WON'T FEEL THE NEED FOR DAILY MEDITATIVE COMMUNION WITH CHRIST.

Personal worship is not first about how many times you have read through your Bible. It is not about once again working yourself through your favorite devotional or commentary. It is not about going back over your sermon notes. All of these things must be seen and used as aids for a more foundational thing. What is this thing? It is the humble, daily, personal, meditative, joyful worship of God. It is beginning or ending your day with communion with Christ. It is the regular habit of "gazing up at the beauty of the Lord" (see Ps. 27:4).

Communion with Christ is fueled by humility. Communion with Christ is fueled by sadness and celebration. Communion with Christ is propelled by an accurate sense of who you are and what you need, and a celebration of the One who gives it. Awareness of sin and the promise of salvation are what daily drive you to Christ, not to rush through a passage in his Word and say a quick prayer but to sit at his feet and grieve your sin and give praise for the grace that meets you in it. Assessments of arrival crush personal worship.

6) YOU WILL TAKE CREDIT FOR SUCCESSES THAT ONLY GRACE CAN PRODUCE.

I've said it already in this chapter: we take too much credit. We give pastors too much credit for what only powerful, divine, sovereign grace has the power to accomplish. Then having given the instrument too much credit, we run to the conference or buy the book so that we can do what our ministry hero has done. Can we learn from others? Of course. Can ingredients of a healthy ministry be identified? Yes. Should we be thankful for dedicated servants of the Lord and communicate our thanks? It would be wrong not to. But we must reserve our adoration (whether of self or of another) for the Lord. We cannot remind ourselves enough that without his presence, power, and grace, our ministries are nothing. This is the inescapable bottom line.

7) YOU WILL FEEL ENTITLED TO WHAT YOU COULD NEVER EARN OR ACHIEVE.

Entitlement always seems to follow pride. If you think you've earned ________, then you will think you deserve ________. Then, carrying around not only pride but also entitlement, you will tend to turn blessings into demands and gifts of grace into what is to be expected. We must never forget that we have earned neither our standing with the Lord nor our place in ministry. Each moment that he accepts us and each situation in which he uses us are the result of one thing and one thing alone: grace. We have no right before God or others to self-assuredly stand with our hands out. We are independently entitled to nothing but his anger; it is only grace that entitles us to his accepting love. The smug expectation of blessing will cause you to question not only the appreciation of the people around you but also the goodness of God.

8) YOU WILL BE LESS THAN WATCHFUL AND PROTECTIVE WHEN IT COMES TO TEMPTATION AND SIN.

Arrival causes you to be too self-assured; being self-assured causes you to make unwise choices; unwise choices expose you to temptation and sin; pride causes you to think you can handle the exposure—and before long you have fallen. Arrival causes you to forget the daily war that is fought in your heart and to live with a peacetime mentality. Because you think of yourself more highly than you ought to think, you don't build the precautions into your spiritual lifestyle that need to be there. You begin to lose sight of the fact that you are like everyone else that you know or minister to. You live right smack-dab in the middle of the already and the not yet. In the middle there is temptation all around. In the middle you are still susceptible to its draw. In the middle there is still an enemy lurking around looking for his next meal. In the middle we are capable of self-deceit and personal delusion. In the middle we still need to be rescued from ourselves. In the middle we must always live humble, concerned, and protective lives. In the middle we constantly need grace's rescue.

9) YOU WILL LOAD MORE ON YOUR MINISTRY THAN YOU CAN RESPONSIBLY HANDLE.

Pride causes you to accept more responsibility than you can bear. Arrival allows you to assign more ministry work to yourself than you can realistically accomplish. Self-glory causes you to think that you're more essential than you actually are and more necessary than you will ever be. It's pride, not humility, that makes it hard to say no. It's pride that makes it hard to live within the limits of your true character and strength. I am persuaded that much of the tension between family and ministry is caused by arrival. We know that God won't call us to keep one command in a way that would cause us to break another. So if, over the long haul, our family has suffered neglect because of our ministry, it is because we are doing things in ministry that we should not be doing because we have wrongly assessed that we can handle more than we are able to handle.

▲ ▲ ▲

What about you, pastor? Is there evidence of the fruit of arrival in your ministry? Let this chapter generate humble self-assessment. The fact of the matter is that you and I are still a bit of a mess. Yes, by grace we often get it right, but we also often get it completely wrong. There are times when we are the exuberant celebrants of the Lord, and there are others times when we are just full of ourselves. There are times when we are deeply grateful, but there are other times when we feel entitled and are demanding. There are times when we lead with a pastoral heart and other times when we are fearful, self-interested, and political. There are times when, as broken people, we meet people in their brokenness with the gospel; there are other times when in pride we just want people to buck up like we have. There are times when we live and work with God's kingdom in view; there are other times when we love ourselves and have a wonderful plan for our lives.

All of this is to say that the great spiritual war doesn't rage only outside of us; there is ample evidence every day that it still rages inside of us. Gospel-driven, Christ-centered ministry, one that gives grace to those who hear, doesn't start with theological knowledge; no, it starts with a humble heart. It starts with a recognition of your own need and the acknowledgment that you and I are more like than unlike the people to whom God has called us to minister.

PART 3

THE DANGER OF ARRIVAL

(FORGETTING WHO YOU ARE)

CHAPTER TWELVE

SELF-GLORY

Pastoral ministry is always shaped, formed, directed, and driven by worship. Your ministry will be shaped by worship of God or worship of you or, for most of us, a troubling mix of both. Perhaps there is no more powerful, seductive, and deceitful temptation in ministry than self-glory. Perhaps in ministry there is no more potent intoxicant than the praise of men, and there is no more dangerous form of drunkenness than to be drunk with your own glory. It has the power to reduce you to shocking self-righteousness and inapproachability. It will make you someone who is hard to work with, and it will make it nearly impossible for those around you to help you see that you've become hard to work with. It will make you look down on people who are more like you than unlike you. It will cause you to surround yourself with people who too often say yes and too frequently are ready to agree. It will leave you spiritually unwise and morally unprotected. And all of this will happen without your notice because you will remain convinced that you are perfectly okay. When confronted, you will remind yourself of your glory. When questioned, you will defend your glory. You will deny your complicity in problems and your participation in failure. You'll be far too skilled at assigning blame than shouldering blame. You'll be better at controlling than you are at serving. You'll resist work that you think is below you and take offense at those who would presume to tell you what to do. You'll constantly confuse being an ambassador with being a king.

He was a mess, but he didn't know it. His ministry was breaking under the burden, but he didn't see it. His marriage was in a state of constant dysfunction, but he didn't have a clue. He really did live and minister as if he had arrived. In ways to which he seemed blind, he was all too filled with a sense of the glory of his abilities, gifts, insight, experience, and leadership.

When his wife would venture to make even the most mildly critical comment on one of his sermons, he would be highly offended and quickly let her know that she didn't know what she was talking about. When a fellow leader would question one of his proposed initiatives, he was quicker to defend his ideas than he was to listen to the way those ideas were being understood by others. His administrative assistant learned to avoid those areas where he was easily and quickly irritated. He had no time to participate in a small group. He would say to his wife, who longed for them to participate together, "With all that I have on my plate, I don't have time to spend listening to someone do a poor job of leading a Bible study." The guys he once met with he didn't meet with anymore. Yes, he told his congregation again and again that their walk with God was a community project, but he felt little need for that community himself. His sermons lacked pastoral tenderness. They failed to portray a winsome passion for the gospel. They were more self-assured biblical lectures than they were the practically applied exegesis of a man who himself was being broken and encouraged by the grand redemptive story.

He seemed more self-assured than filled with the courage of faith. He seemed more a local-church-advancement idea factory than someone who really did believe that the hope of the church is Christ. He kept calling meetings, but they weren't really formed by his being respectful of the gifts of others. These meetings weren't collaborative; no, they were more gatherings for the purpose of announcements and pronouncements. He would dominate the meeting with his talking and would quickly call his leaders to give support to ideas that were still very fresh in their thinking. He was good at shutting down questions and disarming criticisms, but I must say again, he wouldn't have seen himself this way at all.

He felt burdened by all that he was assigned to do, but he bore that burden because he had loaded too many things on his plate. And he did that because he found it harder and harder to delegate ministry to others. He was convinced that most of the strategic things that needed to be done would be best done by him. Fewer and fewer people were commissioned to do ministry tasks. No, fellow leaders were more and more tasked with support duties because the larger ministry duties were all done by him.

He saw himself as being way more essential to the health of his church than any human being ever is. Because of this, there were times when he cared too much about what people thought of him. Because he thought of himself as essential, he needed others to see him as essential as well, and when they didn't, it haunted him. He would then target those people as those he needed to win. Conversely, there were times when he cared too little about what people thought about him. He was so self-assured that he didn't feel the need to listen well to those whom God had put in his pathway to challenge him personally and to sharpen his ideas and goals. Self-glory will pull you both ways in your ministry relationships.

Because of all this, trust in his ministry began to flag in the hearts of those who worked alongside him. It's hard to trust someone who is too self-assured, too self-aware, too self-congratulatory, too self-important, and too domineering. It's hard to trust someone who speaks much but doesn't listen well. It's hard to trust someone who is quick to critique but does not receive criticism very well. It's hard to trust someone who is confrontational and unapproachable at the same time. It's hard to trust someone who seems to be more comfortable with taking away ministry than delegating it. It's hard to trust someone who preaches what he appears to think that he doesn't need. It's hard to trust someone who leads by fiat and pronouncement rather than by a biblically informed, gift-recognizing consensus. It's hard to trust someone who has assigned to himself way too much glory. But he did. And the sad thing is, he is not alone. There are way too many pastors who do not understand that their ministries are more shaped by self-glory than by the glory of the risen, ever-present, all-sufficient Christ.

By God's rescuing grace, his wife came to the end of herself. She had watched it all happen. She had watched the humble young pastor whom she had married become the proud man whom she now lived with. She had experienced how his being domineering, unapproachable, and self-assured at home had changed their marriage. She knew that people at their church were struggling with his style of leadership. She had lived with the pain of dear friends leaving the church. So one evening in desperation she sat down next to him in the den and told him she just couldn't do it anymore. She told him of the daily pain she felt as she watched what was happening to him and to the church. She told him she didn't know if it was the right thing to do, but she had come to the point where she was unwilling to stand by and let it continue to happen. She had made an appointment with a well-known local pastor and was going to spill her guts. She said, "Dear, if you don't recognize your need for help, I'll recognize it for you and get the help we both need."

At first he was very angry and felt betrayed, but he eventually said he was willing to go with her for help and counsel. It was at this moment that a process of radical rescue and restoration began.

Pastor, what about you? Where in your ministry is there evidence of self-glory? Where are you more dominant than you should be? Where do you fail to listen when you should? Where do you attempt to control things that you don't need to control? Where do you find it hard to delegate ministry to others? Where are you tempted to speak more than you should? Where do you fail to recognize and esteem the gifts of others? Where are you unwilling to examine your weaknesses and admit your failures? Where are you tempted to think of yourself as more essential than you actually are? Where do you care too much about people's respect, esteem, and appreciation? Where do you find it easier to confront than to receive confrontation? Where are you less than thankful for the ministry partners that God has connected you to? Where are you too confident of your own strength and wisdom? Where does self-trust inhibit ministry-forming trust of Christ? Are there ways in which the health of your ministry is being weakened by self-glory?

HUMILITY IN MINISTRY: A CHRISTOLOGICAL MODEL

There is a startling moment in the life of Jesus and the disciples that devastates self-glory and defines the kind of humility that, by grace, should grip the heart of every pastor and form the lifestyle of his ministry.

> Now before the Feast of the Passover, when Jesus knew that his hour had come to depart out of this world to the Father, having loved his own who were in the world, he loved them to the end. During supper, when the devil had already put it into the heart of Judas Iscariot, Simon's son, to betray him, Jesus, knowing that the Father had given all things into his hands, and that he had come from God and was going back to God, rose from supper. He laid aside his outer garments, and taking a towel, tied it around his waist. Then he poured water into a basin and began to wash the disciples' feet and to wipe them with the towel that was wrapped around him. He came to Simon Peter, who said to him, "Lord, do you wash my feet?" Jesus answered him, "What I am doing you do not understand now, but afterward you will understand." Peter said to him, "You shall never wash my feet." Jesus answered him, "If I do not wash you, you have no share with me." Simon Peter said to him, "Lord, not my feet only but also my hands and my head!" Jesus said to him, "The one who has bathed does not need to wash, except for his feet, but is completely clean. And you are clean, but not every one of you." For he knew who was to betray him; that was why he said, "Not all of you are clean." When he had washed their feet and put on his outer garments and resumed his place, he said to them, "Do you understand what I have done to you? You call me Teacher and Lord, and you are right, for so I am. If I then, your Lord and Teacher, have washed your feet, you also ought to wash one another's feet. For I have given you an example, that you also should do just as I have done to you. Truly, truly, I say to you, a servant is not greater than his master, nor is a messenger greater than the one who sent him. If you know these things, blessed are you if you do them." (John 13:1–17)

It is one of those moments in the life of Jesus that is so amazing, so counterintuitive, that it is almost impossible to wrap your brain around it, let alone capture it in words. Jesus is in that final moment with his disciples in that rented upper room. It is a holy moment when he declares himself to be the Passover Lamb. Because the room is rented, there is no servant standing by with the requisite pitcher, basin, and towel to wash Jesus's and the disciples' feet. Of course, the disciples, being full of themselves, all too concerned with their power and position in the kingdom, were too proud to do the dirty deed.

Now, this debasing but culturally essential task was not assigned to just any servant. It is clear that in New Testament times there were many levels of authority and responsibility in the culture of servanthood. There were servants who managed whole households, and there were servants who lived the menial life of a slave. The job of washing people's dirty feet before they reclined to eat was reserved for the lowest, most junior, no-account slave. There is no way that the disciples would lower themselves to such a position in front of one another, at least not while they were vying for kingdom greatness.

At the end of the meal, Jesus arises, takes off his outer garments, ties the towel around his waist, and fills the basin with water. He couldn't be about to do what you think he's going to do! This is Lord God Almighty. This is the Son of God, the promised king, the creator of all that is. This One is the fulfillment of all the covenant promises. This is the Savior Lamb. He can't be thinking of doing something so unseemly, so undignified, and so slave-like. But that was exactly his intention. And it is vital to understand that he knew exactly who he was and how this connected to his true identity and mission. John says that Jesus went at this low and dirty task knowing exactly who he was, where he'd come from, and what he was sent to do: "Jesus, knowing that the Father had given all things into his hands, and that he had come from God and was going back to God, rose." This stunning act of humble love resulted not from Jesus's forgetting who he was but from remembering who he was. This was the holy mission of the Son Savior. He had to be willing to enter the lowest human condition, to do the most debased thing, and to let go of his rights of position in order that we might be redeemed. It was a high and holy calling, and it was the only way. His identity, as the Son of God, didn't lead him to be arrogant and entitled, unwilling to do what needed to be done to accomplish redemption. His identity didn't cause him to assess that he was too good for the task. No, his identity motivated and propelled him to do what the disciples were convinced was below them.

When the dirty task had been completed, Jesus looked at his disciples and said, "If I then, your Lord and Teacher, have washed your feet, you also ought to wash one another's feet." Christ is saying, "The attitude I have had toward you, you must have toward one another. My sense of calling must become your sense of calling. The willingness that I have exhibited, you must live out in your ministries." What is that attitude? What is the commitment that must shape the ministry of every pastor?

You and I must not become pastors who are all too aware of our positions. We must not give way to protecting and polishing our power and prominence. We must resist feeling privileged, special, or in a different category. We must not think of ourselves as deserving or entitled. We must not demand to be treated differently or put on some ministry pedestal. We must not minister from above but from alongside.

What is the grand lesson, the grand calling, of this startling moment? Here it is: Jesus says, "If you're not greater than your master, and he has been willing to do this disgusting thing, you must also be willing. If you are my ambassadors, called to represent my will and way, called to be tools of my redeeming grace, then you must not think that any ministry task is beneath you. You must be willing to do the lowest, most debased thing so that my work and my will be done. You must not refuse. You must not think of yourself as too good. You must be willing to be the lowest of slaves in order that my kingdom may come and my will may be done. You must be willing to do whatever is necessary to position yourself as a tool of redeeming grace. You must not be too proud. You must not be unwilling."

Let's be honest, pastors: we are tempted to think of ourselves more highly than we ought to think. At times, we do chafe against things that we think are beneath our pay grade. We are not always willing to do the dirty work of the ministry. I know I'm not always ready and willing. We are too oriented to reputation, position, and power. We do desire to be recognized as prominent. I know I struggle with this. We are not attracted to redemptive servitude. We do want our ministries to be clean and comfortable. I know I do. We do tend to think of ourselves more as movers and shakers than as servants. And all of this is because we don't get our identity as an ambassador. No, if you and I think there is kingdom work that is beneath us, we think that because we are identity amnesiacs. And there is a short step between forgetting our assigned position and inserting ourselves into God's position.

The amazing example and commission of Christ should produce grief that leads to confession in all of us. We do lose our way. We do become more masters than servants. And in our heart of hearts we know that we will never become what we have been called to become unless we are rescued by the very same grace we have come to proclaim and live before others. And we don't have to fear that our silly, delusional, and unearned pride will cause the Father to turn his back on us.

He knows who you are. He knows that you don't measure up. He knows that you still fall short of his righteous requirement; that's why he has given you the gift of his Son. You can run to him and admit to embarrassing self-glory and know that he won't mock you or slap you away, because your standing before him is not based on your performance but on the spotless performance of his Son. Why don't you right here, right now, make the confession that you need to make? Cry for the help you need. Your Savior is near, and he is both willing and able.

THE MINISTRY-DAMAGING FRUIT OF SELF-GLORY

It is important to recognize the harvest of self-glory in you and in your ministry. May God use the following list to give you diagnostic wisdom. May he use it to expose your heart and to redirect your ministry. Here is the ministry-shaping power of self-glory.

1) SELF-GLORY WILL CAUSE YOU TO PARADE IN PUBLIC WHAT SHOULD BE KEPT IN PRIVATE.

The Pharisees live for us as a primary example. Because they saw their lives as glorious, they were quick to parade that glory before the watching eyes of those around them. The more you think you've arrived and the less you see yourself as daily needing rescuing grace, the more you will tend to be self-referencing and self-congratulating. Because you are attentive to self-glory, you will work to get greater glory, even when you aren't aware that you're doing it. You will tend to tell personal stories that make you more the hero than you actually were. You will find ways, in public settings, of talking about private acts of faith. Because you think you are worthy of acclaim, you will seek the acclaim of others by finding ways to present yourself as "godly."

Now, I know most of the pastors reading this will think they would never do this, but I am convinced that there is a whole lot more "righteousness parading" in pastoral ministry than we would tend to think. It is one of the reasons that I find pastors' conferences, presbytery meetings, general assemblies, ministeriums, and church-planting gatherings uncomfortable at times. Around the table after a session, these gatherings can degenerate into a pastoral ministry "spitting contest" where we are at least tempted to be less than honest about what is really going on in our hearts and in our ministries. After celebrating the glory of the grace of the gospel, there is way too much self-congratulatory glory talking by people who seem to need more acclaim than they actually need or deserve.

2) SELF-GLORY WILL CAUSE YOU TO BE WAY TOO SELF-REFERENCING.

We all know it, we've all seen it, we've all been uncomfortable with it, and we've all done it. The bottom line is this: proud people tend to talk about themselves a lot. Proud people tend to like their opinions more than the opinions of others. Proud people think their stories are more interesting and engaging than others. Proud people think they know and understand more than others'. Proud people think they've earned the right to be heard. Proud people think they have glory to offer.

Proud people, because they are basically proud of what they know and of what they've done, talk a lot about both. Proud people don't reference weakness. Proud people don't talk about failure. Proud people don't confess sin. So proud people are better at putting the spotlight on themselves than at shining the light of their stories and opinions on God's glorious and utterly undeserved grace.

3) SELF-GLORY WILL CAUSE YOU TO TALK WHEN YOU SHOULD BE QUIET.

When you think you've arrived, you are quite confident in and proud of your opinions. You trust your opinions more than you trust others', so you are not as interested in the opinions of others as you should be, so you will tend to want your thoughts, perspectives, and viewpoints to win the day in any given meeting or conversation. This means you will be way more comfortable than you should be with dominating a gathering with your talk. You will fail to see that in a multitude of counselors there is wisdom. You will fail to see the essentiality of the ministry of the body of Christ in your life. You will fail to recognize your own bias and spiritual blindness. So you won't come to meetings, formal or informal, with a personal sense of need for what others have to offer, and you will control the talk more than you should.

4) SELF-GLORY WILL CAUSE YOU TO BE QUIET WHEN YOU SHOULD SPEAK.

But self-glory can go the other way as well. Leaders who are too self-confident, who unwittingly attribute to themselves what could only have been accomplished by grace, often see meetings as a waste of time. Because they are proud, they are too independent, so meetings tend to be viewed as an irritating and unhelpful interruption of an already-too-busy ministry schedule. Because of this they will either blow off a meeting or tolerate the gathering, attempting to bring it to a close as quickly as possible. So they don't throw their ideas out for consideration and evaluation because, frankly, they don't think they need it. And when their ideas are on the table and being debated, they don't jump into the fray, because they think that what they have opined or proposed simply doesn't need to be defended. Self-glory really will cause you to speak too much when you should listen and to feel no need to speak when you surely should.

5) SELF-GLORY WILL CAUSE YOU TO CARE TOO MUCH ABOUT WHAT PEOPLE THINK OF YOU.

When you have fallen into thinking that you're something, you want people to recognize the something that you think you are. Again, you see it in the Pharisees; personal assessments of self-glory always lead to glory-seeking behavior of some kind. People who think they've arrived can become all too aware of how others are responding to them. Because you're hypervigilant, watching the way the people in your ministry are responding to your ministry, in ways you are probably not aware of you will begin to shape the things you say and do for the purpose of self-acclaim. You will begin to say and do things in a way that gets you the recognition that you think you deserve. Sadly, you actually begin to fall into ministering the gospel of Jesus Christ not for the glory of Christ or the redemption of the people under your care but for the sake of your own glory. I have done this. I have thought during the preparation for a sermon that a certain point put a certain way would win a detractor, and I have watched certain people's reactions as I have preached. In these moments, in the preparation and preaching of a sermon, I have forsaken my calling as the ambassador of the eternal glory of another for the purpose of my acquiring the temporary praise of men.

6) SELF-GLORY WILL CAUSE YOU TO CARE TOO LITTLE ABOUT WHAT PEOPLE THINK ABOUT YOU.

But this too can go another way. If you think you've arrived, you may go the direction of caring way too little about what people think of you. You are so self-assured that you simply don't think you need to have your thoughts, ideas, actions, words, plans, goals, attitudes, or initiatives evaluated by others. You really don't think you need help. You don't think that what you have to offer will be enhanced or sharpened by the contribution of others. So you again and again do alone what should be done in a group process. And if you work with a group, you will tend to surround yourself with people who are all too impressed with you and all too excited to be included by you, and who will find it hard to say anything to you but yes. You have forgotten who you are and what your Savior says you daily need and are: living in a place of both personal and ministry danger.

7) SELF-GLORY WILL CAUSE YOU TO RESIST FACING AND ADMITTING YOUR SINS, WEAKNESSES, AND FAILURES.

Why do any of us get upset or tense when confronted? Why do any of us activate our inner lawyer and rise to our own defense? Why do any of us turn the tables and remind the other person that we are not the only sinner in the room? Why do we argue about the facts or dispute the other person's interpretation? We do all of these things because we are convinced in our hearts that we are more righteous than how we are being portrayed in this moment of confrontation. Proud people don't welcome loving warning, rebuke, confrontation, question, criticism, or accountability, because they don't feel the need for it. And when they do fail, they are very good at erecting plausible reasons for what they said or did, given the stresses of the situation or relationship in which it was done.

Pastor, are you quick to admit weakness? Are you ready to own your failures before God and others? Are you ready to face your weaknesses with humility? Remember, pastor, if the eyes or ears of a ministry partner ever see or hear your sin, weakness, or failure, it is never a hassle, it is never a ministry interruption, and it should never be viewed as an affront. It is always grace. God loves you, and he has put you in this community of faith, and he will reveal your personal spiritual needs to those around you so that they may be his tools of conviction, rescue, and transformation.

8) SELF-GLORY WILL CAUSE YOU TO STRUGGLE WITH THE BLESSINGS OF OTHERS.

Self-glory is always at the base of envy. You are envious of the blessings of others because you see them as less deserving than you are.

And because you see yourself as more deserving, it is hard not to be mad that they got what you deserve, and it is nearly impossible not to crave and covet what they are wrongfully enjoying. In your envious self-glory you are actually charging God with being unjust and unfair. In ways you may not be aware of, you begin to be comfortable with doubting God's wisdom, justice, and goodness. You don't think he has been kind to you in the way that you deserve. This begins to rob you of motivation to do what is right, because it doesn't seem to make any difference.

It is important to recognize that there is a short step between envy and bitterness. That's why envious Asaph cries in Psalm 73, "All in vain have I kept my heart clean and washed my hands in innocence" (v. 13). He's saying, "I've obeyed, and this is what I get?" Then he writes, "When my soul was embittered, when I was pricked in heart, I was brutish and ignorant; I was like a beast toward you" (vv. 21–22). What a word picture—a bitter beast! I have met many bitter pastors, men who are convinced that they've endured hardships that they really didn't deserve. I have met many bitter pastors, envious of the ministries of others, who have lost their motivation and their joy and are heartlessly cranking out ministry week after week. I have met many pastors who have come to doubt the goodness of God, and, tragically, they don't tend to run for help in their time of need to someone they've come to doubt.

9) SELF-GLORY WILL CAUSE YOU TO BE MORE POSITION ORIENTED THAN SUBMISSION ORIENTED.

Self-glory will always make you more oriented to place, power, and position than to how submission to a greater King is worked out in the context of your ministry. You see this in the lives of the disciples. Jesus hadn't called them to himself to make their little-kingdom purposes come true but to welcome them as recipients and instruments of the work of a better kingdom. Yet, in their pride, they missed the whole point and were all too perseveringly oriented to the question of who would be greatest in the kingdom.

You can never fulfill your ambassadorial calling and at the same time want the power and position of a king. Position orientation will cause you to be political when you should be pastoral. It will cause you to require service when you should be willing to serve. It will cause you to demand of others what you wouldn't be willing to do yourself. It will cause you to ask for privilege when you should be willing to give up your rights. It will cause you to think too much about how things will affect you rather than about how things will reflect on Christ. It will cause you to want to set the agenda rather than to find joy in submitting to the agenda of Another. Self-glory turns chosen and called ambassadors into self-appointed kings. And when this happens, in ways you and I might not be aware of, we are ministering to promote a person, but that person just doesn't happen to be Jesus Christ.

10) SELF-GLORY WILL CAUSE YOU TO CONTROL MINISTRY RATHER THAN DELEGATE MINISTRY.

You, when you are full of yourself, when you are too self-assured, will tend to think that you're the most capable person in the circle of your ministry. You will find it hard to recognize and esteem the God-given gifts of others, and because you don't, you will find it hard to make your ministry a community process. Thinking of yourself more highly than you ought to think always leads to looking down on others in some way. It is personal humility and neediness that will cause you to seek out and esteem the gifts and contributions of others. Pastors who think that they've arrived don't tend to like group process and tend to see delegation as a bit of a waste of time. In their hearts they think, *Why should I give to another what I could do better myself*? Pastoral pride will crush shared ministry and the essential ministry of the body of Christ.

▲ ▲ ▲

It is important to say that I have written the above section with personal grief and remorse. In shocking self-glory I have fallen, at some times in my ministry, into all of these traps. I have dominated when I should have listened. I have controlled what I should have given to others. I have been defensive when I desperately needed rebuke. I have resisted help when I should have been crying out for it. I have been too full of my own opinion and too dismissive of the perspective of others. I have paraded my stuff for the approval of others. I am sad as I reflect on my many years of ministry, but I am not depressed. I am not, because in all of my weakness, the God of amazing grace has rescued and restored again and again. He has progressively delivered me from me (a work that is still going on). And in being torn between the kingdom of self and the kingdom of God, he has miraculously used me in the lives of many. In love, he has worked to dent and deface my glory so that his glory would be my delight. He has plundered my kingdom so that his kingdom would be my joy. And he has crushed my crown under his feet so that I would quest to be a good ambassador and not crave to be a king.

In this violent mercy there is hope for every person in ministry. Your Lord is not just after the success of your ministry; he is working to dethrone you as well. It is only when his throne is more important than yours that you will find joy in the hard and humbling task of gospel ministry. And his grace will not relent until our hearts have been fully captured by his glory. Now, that's good news!

CHAPTER THIRTEEN

ALWAYS PREPARING

I will confess that I am a bit obsessed. It is very hard for me to turn off my mind. I will often pull off the road while driving or stop in the middle of a walk to pull out my phone and take notes because thoughts that I've been carrying around with me have suddenly taken shape. My wife, Luella, complains often that even though I am with her physically, it seems that I'm not really there. She can tell by my quietness or by the look on my face that my mind and attention have been kidnapped by the content of something I am working on. I have always found it very hard to escape the rule of "King Preparation." On my days off I find it very hard to be off and to turn off. I think that I'm incessantly distracted by what God has called me to do. I think that I seldom ever truly step away from ministry into my private life. I may be silent, and I may be in a place of quiet, but the noise of ministry is loud in my head. I think there are ways in which I never stop preparing.

The other day I was very aware of the battle between preparation and personal devotion that takes place in my heart. I was facing a rather significant international conference where I was to speak multiple times. I was in the middle of the preparation of new material and the recasting of material previously prepared. I knew that what I was going to say to the people who would come would offer them a new way of thinking about themselves and what it means to walk with God. It was exciting, and I wanted to get it right. As I got out of bed morning after morning, I was tossing around in my head ways of approaching the topic. My day hadn't even had a chance to start, and I had already been kidnapped by the burden of preparation. On my exercise bike, my mind would race faster than my legs as it zoomed from concept to concept, from illustration to illustration, and from application to application. Day after day, as I sat down to read and pray for the nurture of my own soul, the things that I was reading would quickly become new points for the talks to come.

Then at one moment it hit me that I was not reading with myself in view but, rather, with my future hearers. I wasn't being informed, confronted, grieved, or transformed by the passage. In fact, the passage had made minimal impact on me. That morning I was excited about the Scriptures, but not personally, not because I had looked into the mirror of the Word of God and been humbled by what I saw. No, I was excited because I had acquired more content to share with others. There was no personal worship that morning. There was no hunger after God. There was no grief over sin. There was no celebration of grace. There was no movement in my commitment to live by faith. There was no growth in my discipline, perseverance, or hope. There was no awe at the glory of God. There was no deeper sense of his presence and love. There was no deepening of my gratitude for being included in his family. There was no motivating vision of the ultimate defeat of sin. There was no stimulation of my cry for eternity. There was no plea for his kingdom to come and his will to be done.

No, there was no "me" in that moment of personal worship. Maybe it is more correct to say that this moment I have described, even though it took place when I normally have my private time with the Lord, was not a moment of personal worship. There was little about it that was personal or relational. It was not a moment of a child communing with his father. If it was relational in any way, it was more me relating to my future audience than it was me relating to God. I think all preparation to preach or teach should be devotional, but in this instance, preparation crushed devotion. Even though I had the Bible in my hands, my needy and hungry soul was not fed. I walked out of that quiet room personally unchanged, and I realized what had happened only later when I reflected on the morning. Later that day someone asked me what I had been reading in my private time of worship. It was as I answered that I realized I had not had a private time of worship that day; no, just another opportunity to prepare.

I think the struggle I am describing here is a struggle for all of us in ministry. It is very difficult to have the responsibility to preach or teach God's Word each week and not have this responsibility dominate your mind every time you have the Bible in your hands. The commitment to a regular time of communion with your Lord stimulates the battle in your heart between the essentiality of private worship and the necessity of adequate preparation. In God's plan these are not mutually exclusive, nor do they compete with one another. As I have said often, God will not call us to a task that would necessitate our disobeying him in another area. Yet it is very difficult to keep these two aspects of your calling in their proper place.

When I talk to a group of pastors about the lack of private personal worship, I am often looking out at a group of men with their heads down. Many of my listeners have confessed that they cannot remember when their devotional time was consistent and vibrant. Many of them have told me that they have just quit trying to fight the battle. They get up, get themselves ready, and jump in the ministry saddle. They're ready to jump in to serve Jesus; they just have little personal time to spend with him in a life of urgent ministry demands. They live with Jesus like husbands who provide well for their wives but have little time left to participate in a relationship that is remotely intimate. They provide well, but they don't love well. They work hard but not at the primary relationship of their lives. Many pastors out there are seeking to lead and teach well, but it is simply not fueled or directed by the devotion of their hearts to their Savior. Their Christianity is more an institutional discipline than a personal relationship. They are more drawn to ideas than to Jesus. They are more drawn to ministry success than to personal growth. The next phase of the strategic plan fills their eyes more than the glory of God and the grandeur of his grace. They have lost the center of it all, and their hearts have been kidnapped, and many of them don't know it.

But there is another thing that comes in play here. The lack of a meditative, Christ-centered devotional life in many pastors is not just the result of the seemingly unending demands of ministry preparation; it is also the product of arrival. I am convinced that when busyness intersects with arrival, one of the first things that goes is private worship. Perhaps it is a combination of fear and gratitude that drives us to our knees and into communion with Christ each morning. It is when we face who we are and the fickleness of our hearts that we feel the need to have our hearts recaptured morning after morning. It is when we reflect on the fact that sin is not always a horror to us but sometimes appears positively attractive that we want to run into the protective arms of our Lord again and again. It is when we consider the dangerous temptation of this fallen world that we will want to get help for the battle day after day. It is fear of our own weaknesses that drives us to the Savior for strength. It is when we fear the power of the foolishness that still remains in us that we are propelled to daily seek the wisdom that can be found only in the pages of Scripture. A humble and holy fear is a major part of what propels a consistent life of daily personal worship.

So when you've forgotten who you are, when you assign to yourself more maturity than you actually have, and when you think you are more capable than you really are, you leave yourself little reason to seek the ongoing help of your Savior.

Arrival also crushes the gratitude that fuels personal worship. It bears repeating that when you think you've arrived, you congratulate yourself for things in yourself that only grace could produce. When you think you've arrived, you tend to take credit for things that only God could have produced. You begin to think that success in ministry has more to do with you than it actually does. You begin to think you're more essential than you really are. None of this produces the gratitude that fuels worship. Proud people tend not to be thankful, precisely because pride causes them to take more credit than they deserve.

So when ministry skill, experience, and success begin to redefine the way you think about you, what inevitably weakens is your zeal for personal worship. Because you are convinced that you're well, you feel little real need for the care, comfort, wisdom, and healing of the Great Physician. The humble hunger of fear and the celebratory hunger of gratitude have been crushed by arrival, and worship is what takes the hit.

Perhaps one of the silent scandals of the modern evangelical church is that there are many, many pastors in this place. They are leaders of gospel ministries, but they have little felt need for the gospel in their daily lives. They are not concerned for the healing, nurture, and growth of their own hearts. They are not constantly thankful for rescuing, transforming, and enabling grace. They are functionally more in love with ministry than they are in love with Christ. They are more excited about the ideas of redemption than they are about the Redeemer. Whether they know it or not, they have come to be more impressed with themselves than they are with the One who gives them both physical and spiritual breath. They don't live with the daily grief of knowing that everything they teach is much easier to teach than to live. They aren't sad that they often fail to be good ambassadors of the King. They fail to recognize the artifacts of the old way in their hearts—impatience, anger, bitterness, lust, envy, greed, self-righteousness, etc.—and they don't long for the gracious, character-shaping hands of the Redeemer to be on them. They neglect consistent habits of personal worship not because they are undisciplined or lazy; it's because they need to prepare for some upcoming ministry responsibility. They're not motivated to spend time in personal worship and meditation because arrival has crushed the godly fear and the humble gratitude that make it happen.

THE DANGEROUS DICHOTOMY

All of this buys into a dangerous and fallacious dichotomy. It is the belief, whether conscious or not, that my private and ministry lives are not intimately and causally connected. It is beginning to believe that a man who has no personal life of worship can lead people to worship God. It is believing that a person who lacks vertical gratitude can lead others to be thankful. It is believing that a proud person is qualified to lead a congregation to be humble. It is the thought that you can give away in ministry that which you do not have.

But the New Testament has no place for a pastor's ever beginning to believe that he is two separate people: the private man at home and the public man in the pulpit. Paul would have considered this a very dangerous pastoral-ministry heresy. So when Paul lays out the qualifications for eldership, one of the places he tells you to go and look is the pastor's home. If an elder cannot manage his home well, how can he lead the local body of believers that is under his care?

You are one person. The boundaries of life and ministry are not separate and defined. You do not become a different person when you step into some kind of ministry function. You and I are each in possession of only one heart, so the condition of our heart is a huge issue in our ministry. I know this seems blatantly obvious, but I'm afraid it is not so functionally obvious in our churches.

Hear Paul's counsel to young pastor Timothy: "Keep a close watch on yourself and on the teaching. Persist in this, for by so doing you will save both yourself and your hearers" (1 Tim. 4:16). There are two crucial assumptions behind Paul's counsel to Timothy. The first is that Timothy had not arrived. Paul is reminding Timothy that as a pastor he must remember that he is in the middle of his own sanctification. He must remember that his heart is still capable of wandering. He must remember that he needs everything that he would offer to others. He needs warning, encouragement, rebuke, counsel, etc. Timothy, the minister of the gospel, personally needs the gospel as well. So Paul's advice is for Timothy to keep a close watch on himself. Embedded in this warning to Timothy is a call to nurture his own heart. He cannot allow himself to think that all he needs to do to be useful in ministry is prepare well, and he cannot let personal nurture be crushed by the demands of preparation. Yes, he must prepare and prepare well. He must have a careful eye on his teaching, but that alone is simply not enough.

So, Paul's first assumption is that because of remaining sin, Timothy is still in danger and must keep a humble eye on his own heart. But Paul follows this with a second assumption that is important not to miss. It is that Timothy's guarding and nurturing his heart is not only for his own protection and growth but also for the salvation of his hearers. Paul is assuming that the condition of Timothy's heart will somehow, someway shape the direction and fruitfulness of his ministry.

The private nurture of your own heart as a pastor is not only a humble confession of need and a confession of your love for your Savior; it is also a statement of your love for the people that God has placed in your care. It is in this way that preparation and personal devotion intersect. No, you are not reading that passage in the morning to develop content for a moment of teaching; you're reading it to feed your own heart. But in so doing, you are preparing your heart to face all the responsibilities, opportunities, and temptations of local-church ministry. What you are doing morning after morning raises the potential that in crucial moments of pastoral ministry you will be part of what God is doing rather than in the way of it.

You see, there are very important moments in local-church ministry when the church is blessed and protected not because the person leading knows all the right things but because that person brings the right heart to the moment. So he is able to deal wisely with accusation, or patiently with those who want to control, or humbly with those who idolize him more than they should. He is not just prepared to teach but also to navigate the land mines of temptation that are at the feet of everyone who ministers to fallen people in this flawed world. If you daily work to guard your heart, you are at the same time making a daily commitment to pastor and protect your people. The two simply cannot be separated. And when arrival weakens your need to guard your own heart, you put the people whom God has called you to pastor in danger as well.

PRIVATE WORSHIP: YOUR DEATH, YOUR LIFE

It really is true: the health and success of your ministry really are a matter of death and life. If you are ever going to be an ambassador in the hands of a God of glorious and powerful grace, you must die. You must die to your plans for your own life. You must die to your self-focused dreams of success. You must die to your demands for comfort and ease. You must die to your individual definition of the good life.

You must die to your demands for pleasure, acclaim, prominence, and respect. You must die to your desire to be in control. You must die to your hope for independent righteousness. You must die to your plans for others. You must die to your craving for a certain lifestyle or that particular location. You must die to your own kingship. You must die to the pursuit of your own glory in order to take up the cause of the glory of Another. You must die to your control over your own time. You must die to your maintenance of your reputation. You must die to having the final answer and getting your own way. You must die to your unfaltering confidence in you. You must die.

What does this have to do with your life of private personal worship? Well, here it is. Your private devotional life has the power to kill you like nothing else does. By "kill you," I mean that it has the power to kill the "me-ism" that is inside you (and me) that will again and again cause you to be in the way of, rather than part of, whatever it is that God is doing at the moment. Private personal worship is an effective tool of grace in the hands of God to kill those things in you that must die in order that you be what you have been called to be and do what you have been appointed to do in your place of ministry. Let me explain.

First, consistent personal worship will result in your having an *accurate view of God.* One of the great dangers for all of us is this: we have the perverse ability to look around and not see the amazing glory of God. Even though, as Isaiah put it, "the whole earth is full of his glory" (Isa. 6:3), we can be incredibly blind to the display that is everywhere around us. Our view gets clouded by all the other things in the paths of our sight. We see all of those troubled people in desperate need of pastoral care. We see a church budget that doesn't seem to be working. We see leaders that need to function with greater humility and unity. We see a facility that is beyond its usefulness. We see a children's ministry that is languishing, devoid of effective leadership. We see places of theological division and controversy. We see the worship leader who is more performer than pastor. We see series of sermons that need to be prepared, missionaries that need to be supported, and leaders that need to be trained. The eyes of our hearts are filled with many important things, but often we don't see the most important thing.

Daily Bible study, meditation, and prayer have the power and potential to make the glory of God big in our eyes once again. And if we are daily confronted with his grandeur, not only will that give us courage and hope but also it will work to remind us that we are neither grand nor glorious. Personal worship has the power to progressively put us in our place. Because it puts God at the center of the universe, it has the power to kill any hope we have of being in the center. Because worship points us to God's wonderful kingdom, it has the power to free us from the bondage of establishing our own. Because private worship exposes us again and again to God's life-altering grace, it frees us from our hope that we can change people. Personal worship is one of the things God uses to free us from any remaining trust we have that we can do what only the Messiah is able to do. But it does more.

A private devotional life also gives you an *accurate view of the world.* As day after day the pages of Scripture expose you to the blood and guts, smoke and dirt, of this fallen world, you are progressively freed from your hope that your fallen world, flawed people, or church will ever be the ministry paradise it will never be. You begin to die to unrealistic expectations and pastoral pipe dreams. You are progressively freed from envying the ministry of others and wondering why things are so hard at your post. You begin to understand that ministry is war and that you cannot approach it with a peacetime mentality. You begin to understand that this is not meant to be a destination but that all the struggles of life and ministry in the here and now are meant to prepare you and your people for a final destination. Daily personal worship has the power to free you from the naive and romantic views of the local church that, sadly, often are what people get excited about in ministry. The stark and descriptive honesty of the Bible, as it looks at the world in which you and I live and minister, has the power to kill your selfish dream that you will be able to serve your crucified King without suffering yourself. But there is yet even more.

Private, personal worship has the power to kill our often *inaccurate view of ourselves.* When we daily look into a mirror, we end up with a current and accurate view of ourselves. We would like to think that we know ourselves well. We would like to think that we have a valid estimation of our strengths and weaknesses. We would like to think that we have interpreted our journey appropriately. We would like to think that we have been freed of pointing the finger when we should have taken the blame. We would like to think that we quickly recognize and admit our wrongs, but these things are not always true of us. We often have a very distorted view of ourselves. We often think we are better than we really are. So we desperately need a mirror that will show us ourselves with complete accuracy.

This is important because autonomy, self-reliance, and self-righteousness crush tender, humble, gracious, patient, loving pastoral ministry.

As a pastor you need the hope and courage that only *an accurate view of God's grace* can give you. You need to remember that you don't have to attempt to do in your ministry what only that grace has the power to do. Now, I'm afraid that many pastors lose sight of that grace. I'm afraid they fall into the problem of the army of Israel who compared their potential to the size of themselves and the size of the problem. No wonder they were afraid to face Goliath on the field of battle! They forgot that they were not alone. They forgot that as God's children, their potential was hugely greater than their wisdom, strength, or experience, because Almighty God had covenantally committed himself to unleash his power in their defense.

In the same way, pastors are tempted to mismeasure their potential because, although they probably don't realize it, they have a huge gap in the middle of their understanding of the gospel. They neglect to preach the gospel of the right-here, right-now grace of Jesus Christ to themselves. So they are either afraid to face what they think is beyond their ability, or they assign to themselves abilities they do not have. The page-after-page message of grace that the Bible gives you has the power to kill both paralyzing fear and potential puffing pride, and every pastor needs to daily confess his need of that grace, or he is a danger to himself and becomes a danger to others. That message of grace humbles you and gives you hope at the very same time—two indispensible character qualities for any leader in the church of Jesus Christ.

What kills you also gives you life. As personal worship becomes a gracious tool of your death, progressively causing you to die to your self-reliance, self-righteousness, self-sovereignty, and self-focus, you begin to live, really live. Real life is on the other side of your death. Perhaps true righteousness only ever begins when you come to the end of yourself. Remember the words of Christ: "If anyone would come after me, let him deny himself and take up his cross and follow me. For whoever would save his life will lose it, but whoever loses his life for my sake will find it" (Matt. 16:24–25).

Because daily private worship puts the glory of God in front of me again and again, because it forces me to face the sad condition of my world, because it confronts me with my weaknesses and sin, and because it showers me with God's amazing grace, it progressively makes me *alert and ready* for the things that God has called me to do and for the struggles I will face as I do them.

Private worship is one of God's means of rescuing not just you but also those he has placed in your care. It is a sad and dangerous thing, not just for you but for the church under your care, when assessments of arrival have separated you from the holy fear and humble gratitude that fuel consistent personal worship.

SIGNS THAT YOU'VE FORGOTTEN YOUR DUAL IDENTITY

So, here's the bottom line for anyone in ministry: you must always be careful to carry a dual identity with you, no matter where you are or what you are doing. No matter how influential you become, no matter how well you are known, and no matter how experienced you are, you must fight to hold onto both identities. You must think of yourself not only as an *instrument* of the work but also as a *recipient*. Your work as an instrument does not cancel out your identity as a recipient, and your identity as a recipient doesn't weaken your work as an instrument. You and I must never approach grace only as instruments of that grace in the lives of others; we must also remember that there is no grace that we offer to others that we don't at once need ourselves.

When you forget that you still need to receive what you are called to give others, you quit being a seeker after the grace that is your protection, wisdom, hope, and strength. Forgetting that you are still a needy recipient and thinking of yourself only as an instrument will crush your world of personal study of the Word and your worship of your Lord. It will mean that you quit seeing the Word as for you, and because you do, each time you pick up your Bible it will be for the purpose of preparing to teach others and not for the purpose of nurturing your own heart. In reality, you will be always preparing but not personally consuming the nutrient truths that you are preparing to give to others.

It calls to mind the evocative words of Peter: "Like newborn infants, long for the pure spiritual milk, that by it you may grow up into salvation" (1 Pet. 2:2). I remember the ravenous hunger of our first little boy. He craved the milk that only his mother could provide, and he would not be deterred! But I also remember that after he had satiated his physical hunger, he cried when his mother pulled him away from her chest to put him down. Those tears depicted another hunger. He was also hungry for the intimate connection, communion, and safety of his mother's arms. This provokes me to question myself. Have I lost my infant-like hunger for the nutrition of God's Word? Have I lost my hunger for the comfort and safety of intimate communion with my Lord? Has it all become little more than a disciplined commitment to the service of a religious institution? Has it all been reduced to theological ideas and ministry strategies? Has it quit being a personal relationship with a personal calling and become little more than a job, a career? Has a sincere desire to bring the gospel of grace to others morphed into a dangerous and soul-deadening identity amnesia?

Are you so busy feeding others that you are neglecting the need to feed yourself?

Here are some signs that you can look for in your life and ministry that indicate your work as an *instrument* of grace has caused you to forget or deny your identity as a *recipient* of that same grace.

1) THE BIBLE HAS CEASED BEING A MIRROR.

The first sign is a change in your relationship to the Word of God. *The Bible has ceased being a mirror for you and is used only as a tool for ministry to others.* It is a dangerous place to be; it puts your heart at risk, but this is the place where many, many pastors work and live. It's possible for your life of worship to change as well.

2) WORSHIP MORPHS FROM PRIVATE QUEST TO PUBLIC DUTY.

Worship morphs from a humble and grateful private quest to something you lead as a public duty. Yes, it is your duty to lead others in worship, as it is your duty to teach them from God's Word, but how can you winsomely and persuasively lead people to do what is foreign to your daily experience?

3) CHRISTIANITY BECOMES A SYSTEM RATHER THAN A RELATIONSHIP.

Your Christianity becomes *more about a system of redemption than about a personal relationship and communion with the Redeemer.* Perhaps there is more Christless Christianity out there than we think, and perhaps its existence is first a matter of the heart before it's a weakness in our functional theology.

4) YOUR DESIRE TO MASTER CONTENT IS NOT COUPLED WITH CRAVING.

Another sign of the loss of your recipient identity is that *your desire to master content of the Word is not coupled with a craving that your heart would be mastered by the God of the Word.* One of the dangers of arrival is a subtle bibliolatry where confidence in the God of the Word gets progressively replaced by your confidence in your knowledge and ability to handle the Word. You are more driven to be theologically informed than to have your heart and life radically transformed by

God's Word. Could it be that you have a heart for the Word (a quest for theological expertise and biblical literacy) but not a heart for the God of the Word?

5) YOU HAVE MORE CONCERN FOR THE SIN OF OTHERS THAN FOR YOUR OWN.

Forgetting your recipient identity will also result in you having a *concern for others that overwhelms grief for yourself.* Who of us has not sat in front of a gifted preacher and been listening for someone else? You're not personally hungry and grateful as you listen. No, you're very thankful that so-and-so is in the room because he really needs to hear what the preacher is saying. This dynamic is a real and present temptation for anyone in ministry. You are in great danger if the grief you experience over the condition of others is greater than the grief you feel for your own sin.

6) THE PRIDE OF KNOWING REPLACES THE HUMILITY OF BEING KNOWN.

One final sign of forgetting your two-sided identity: *pride of knowing replaces the humility of being known.* Your life and ministry begin to be shaped more by your pride in what you know than by the humility of being completely known yet fully loved by the Savior. So you minister as one who has arrived rather than as one who still celebrates the rescue of grace that, along with others, he continues to need.

▲ ▲ ▲

Are these signs in your life and ministry? Is there evidence that your call to minister grace has caused you to forget your own need for grace?

One of the sweetest blessings of the cross of Jesus Christ is that the curtain of separation has been torn in two. No longer are the holy places open only to the high priest once a year. No, now each of God's children has been welcomed to come with confidence into God's presence, and not just once a year. When the author of Hebrews writes of this welcome, he then turns and says, "Let us then with confidence draw near . . ." (4:16). We, with all of our sin, weakness, and failures, are welcome to do what should blow our minds. We are not only tolerated by God at a distance; no, we are welcomed into intimate personal communion with the King of kings, the Lord of lords, the creator, the sovereign, the Savior. We, as unholy as we are, are told to go with confidence into his holy presence. The blood of Jesus has made the impossible possible. For the writer of Hebrews there is only one right response to the access we now have to God through Jesus Christ. Here it is: "Draw near." Perhaps, in forgetting who we are and what we have been given, we have essentially quit drawing near. So convinced that we are okay and so busy preparing, many of us have quit communing with the One who is our life, peace, reconciliation, wisdom, hope, forgiveness, and strength. And because we have, the tenderness, humility, patience, and passion that needy and grateful worship produces in our hearts are absent in our ministries.

You simply cannot be a good ambassador of the grace of the King without recognizing your need for the King in your own life. Public ministry is meant to be fueled and propelled by private devotion. When this is absent, you and your ministry change in ways that are potentially harmful to you and to the people you have been called to serve.

Pastor, have arrival and ministry busyness crushed your life of private, meditative, Christ-communing worship? Or, in the words of Hebrews, are you still drawing near?

CHAPTER FOURTEEN

SEPARATION

It was a funny, uncomfortable, yet helpful moment. My assistant Steve and I were sitting with a group of pastors who had asked to have lunch with us. One of the pastors had asked Steve what had motivated him to leave his insurance business to his son-in-law to operate and to make his daily full-time work Paul Tripp Ministries. Spontaneously Steve said, "Well, I don't do what I do for the ministry because I idolize Paul, because Paul can be a bit of a jerk. I do it because I believe in Paul's passion for connecting the transforming power of Jesus Christ to everyday life." As I listened, my first defensive and unspoken response was, "Yes, Steve, I am a jerk at times, but if it is to be announced to pastors, I would like to do the announcing." It was an interesting scene. Some of the pastors laughed; some of them had an uncomfortable look on their faces as I pondered if I should respond to the moment.

The fact is that Steve was exactly right. He has seen me in my most embarrassing, easily irritated, oh-poor-me, hard-to-get-along-with moments. You cannot live and work next to someone without seeing the empirical evidence of the remaining artifacts of his depravity, those things in the heart that still need the transforming hand of the Redeemer. Steve has long since forsaken the delusion that I'm a heroic example of the things I teach. If he was doing what he's doing in ministry for me, by now I would have given him ample reason to quit. I am still a broken man in need of more attention by the restorative hands of grace.

So as we near the end of this book, I want to be brutally honest and ask you to do the same as well. Pastors, we're all still a bit of a mess. We're all at times very poor examples of the truths we teach. We all have the dark ability to expound a passage that lauds God's grace yet be a husband or father of ungrace in the car on the way home. You can lead a men's ministry discussion on the issue of biblical sexual purity and lust at the women in the grocery store on the way home. You can teach about the self-sacrificing nature of love and be self-centered and unwilling to serve at home. You and I can define biblical humility but be proud of what we know and what we've accomplished. You and I have the ability to talk of what it means to invest our gifts and strengths in the work of the kingdom of God and then go home and waste countless hours in front of the flat screen. We talk about the beauty of forgiveness yet harbor bitterness against families or leaders that have opposed us. We are capable of talking about God's ownership of every area of our lives and then masturbate in the bathroom before we go to bed. We talk of the rest we have in God's control and then anxiously work politically behind the scenes to ensure that we get our own way. We talk of giving God the glory that is his due, and then we fudge the numbers to make our ministries look more successful in the eyes of others than they actually are. We talk of trusting God's provision but then get ourselves in debt by spending more than he has provided. We teach people the rest that can be found when you get your identity vertically, but when the rubber meets the road in daily ministry, we care too much about what people think of us. We can teach well what it looks like to be content, but we quickly grumble and complain when the going gets hard. We talk about a heart for ministry, but when we get home all we want is to be left alone. We are all capable of being self-righteous, proud, judgmental, controlling, easily angered, bitter, and demanding. We sometimes act as if we're entitled to our blessings. We often forget how much we need everything we teach. We give evidence every day that we are people in the middle of our own sanctification, that we still need the moment-by-moment rescue of grace.

There is a way in which all of us have a separation in our lives between our more pristine public ministry persona and the more messy details of our private lives. Aspects of this separation will be with us until the Lord returns.

This separation does not necessarily disqualify you from ministry, but it becomes spiritually debilitating to you and your ministry when you become comfortable with it. It is dangerous when you have learned the craft of making this separation work. It is a pastoral disaster when you have conquered the dark spiritual skill of sectoring your own heart, where it's as if you are two separate people and the dark side doesn't haunt you anymore. Remember, this separation exists most frequently in mundane, everyday-life areas. So it is in this context that I must ask, are there areas of clear disharmony or disconnect between your public ministry persona and your private life? And have you become comfortable with the disconnects, even perhaps developing the ability to make them comfortably work?

PREACHING THE GOSPEL TO YOURSELF

It is here that we pastors need to preach the gospel to ourselves. Much of this separation and disharmony is propelled by the fact that in our daily lives we tend to forget the very gospel that we so convincingly preach in public settings to others. Here is the everyday pastoral struggle: not only are we dealing with the reality of our own duplicitous heart, but also there are so many other things that can tug at our heart and in the process begin to shape the things we do and say in ministry.

You can feel the pressure of the expectations for your future in ministry that were placed on you because you did well in seminary. You can feel a weight of responsibility to a denomination that invested in you and in your ministry. You may feel the burden of the vision of long-term and seasoned elders who have had significant impact on the culture and direction of the church. You probably carry the load of your own hopes and dreams for yourself and the vision of what your ministry could be like in the years to come. If you have the heart of a pastor, you feel the weight of the desires, expectations, and spiritual needs of the people God has called you to serve. You feel the responsibility of building the right ministry reputation before the eyes of a watching community. You feel the weight of the obligation to lead a variety of ministries that don't always work in unison. You carry the load of needs of finances and facilities. You face a variety of voices that comment on your public teaching, preaching, and worship leadership. You are drawn into solving problems you didn't create but must be solved. You face the burden of opposition and criticism. You have to deal with leaders who want control and are more political than pastoral. You feel the weight of all these things pulling against the enormous responsibility you have as husband and father.

All of these are legitimate concerns, but together they can result in a heart that is seldom at rest and a ministry that lacks focus, careening from one serious concern to another. There is another thing: it is right to carry the responsibility of all these things, but you must not let any of them rule your heart. All of these concerns can become seductive pastoral idolatries, and when they do, you may think that you are serving God, but your heart is ruled by something to which you have attached your pastoral identity and inner sense of well-being. In your ministry you can faithfully call people to submit their lives to the lordship of Jesus Christ, and in that very same ministry surrender your heart to a whole catalog of pastoral idolatries. When this happens, you do ministry in the hopes of getting horizontally what you have already been given vertically. In ways in which you are unaware, you are asking ministry acclaim, success, reputation, etc., to be your own personal messiah. This will never work. It always leads to bad choices and never results in the inner security that you seek. Think about the insanity of this subtle ministry idolatry.

The people in your congregation did not become active participants in your ministry so that collectively they could make you feel better about yourself and more secure with your ministry gifts. God didn't call you to your particular ministry position so that you could finally cobble together an identity that you could live with. The leadership of the church didn't call you to be their pastor because they knew that you needed a forum where you could find meaning and purpose. The troubled people in your congregation did not come with their troubles so that you could feel needed, essential, and appreciated. The people who faithfully give don't give so that you can build a successful ministry and bask in the security of your accomplishments. So you will never find in your ministry the rest of heart that every human being seeks. And when you look there, it only ends in anxiety, frustration, hurt, disappointment, anger, and bitterness and may ultimately lead you to question the goodness of God. I am convinced that what we often call "ministry burnout" (a term I don't think is particularly helpful) is often the result of pastors' seeking in their ministry what cannot be found there, and because it can't be found there they end up weary and discouraged.

So you have the realities of your private spiritual life colliding with all the responsibilities and expectations of public ministry. You have the danger of becoming comfortable with a disharmony between your public ministry persona and your private spiritual life intersecting with the war of worship that is being fought in your heart as you hear all the idol voices that greet every pastor of every church.

I am afraid that in the heat of this war and in weariness of spiritual battle many pastors give themselves permission to become comfortable with *ministry duplicity* (a separation between the truths they teach and the way they live) and subtle *ministry idolatry* (letting a quest for ________ begin to rule their heart in ministry). The only defense against this is the gospel of Jesus Christ. It is only when we are living out of the life that grace alone is able to give that we quit seeking life elsewhere. It is only when we are embracing the rest of the forgiveness of grace that we can look at ourselves honestly and grieve without wallowing in debilitating guilt and shame.

Pastor, there is no congregation you need to preach to more than yourself. There is no more important place to exegete and expound grace than in your own heart. There is no more important place to teach what it means to apply that grace to the concrete situations, locations, and relationships than in your own life. There is no more important place to fear the harvest of duplicity than in your own heart. There is no place to be more concerned about functional religiously acceptable idolatry than in your own life. Ministry is a war for the gospel in your own heart. Grace enables you to be a good soldier. You and I cannot and must not allow ourselves to become comfortable with things that God says are wrong. You and I must not learn to make things work that simply aren't working. You and I must not work to convince ourselves that our idols aren't really idols. You and I cannot permit ourselves to live a ministry life that lacks consistency and integrity. You and I must understand that we have been called to battle for the gospel of Jesus Christ and that war begins in our hearts.

Let me suggest some vital gospel-in-everyday-life applications that every pastor must preach to himself again and again.

1) I DO NOT HAVE TO BE ANXIOUS THAT I WILL NEVER MEASURE UP, BECAUSE JESUS PERFECTLY MEASURED UP ON MY BEHALF.

Only the gospel can free me from the fear of not being found worthy. The fact of the matter is that I am unworthy. I could never do or say anything that would make me worthy of my Father's acceptance and affection. I could never be so perfectly obedient as to earn his approval. I am not in ministry because, by my own effort, I became a shining example of all that the gospel can produce. I have been freed from the bondage of convincing myself and others that I am worthy. I don't need to privately argue for my worth or do things in public to prove it. Jesus perfectly measured up; he was perfectly worthy on my behalf. He accomplished what was impossible for me to accomplish so that I would be given standing that I did not or could never earn. I don't have to live as if I am still on probation, still being evaluated. I have been accepted, and I have been called into ministry. I have earned neither. Both are gifts of grace. I come into ministry with nothing to prove but this: the gospel of Jesus Christ is reliable and true and has the power to both free and transform you and me. As in ministry, I am faced with both the reality of my own sin and weakness and the pressure of the expectations and criticisms of others. I must preach the gospel of this grace to myself day after day after day.

2) BECAUSE GRACE ALLOWS ME TO GET MY IDENTITY AND SECURITY VERTICALLY, I AM FREED FROM BUILDING THEM ON WHAT PEOPLE THINK OF ME.

There is a way in which, as a pastor, you should care less about what people think about you. Now, here's what I mean: you do not look to them to give you courage, hope, peace, rest, and a reason to continue. As a result, you are freed from being all too attentive to how they respond to you and all too fearful of your detractors. You are in trouble as a pastor when you need regular doses of appreciation and respect in order to continue. Yes, you know you need the ministry of the body of Christ, and you want to be open to that ministry, but you are freed from riding the anxiety-driven roller coaster of people's opinion. Because you have a secure identity as a child of God, you don't need to seek identity from the success of your ministry or from the appreciation of the people around you. This frees you both to be able to listen to criticism without being devastated by it and to be unwilling to let the opinions of others define you and the direction of your ministry. Your secure identity in Christ also allows you to face your weaknesses with humility and honesty. You can do this because your standing with God is not based on your performance but on the perfect obedience of Christ. You need to preach these truths to yourself daily, because in ministry you either seek to get identity from your ministry or stand firm and secure in the identity you have been given in Christ.

3) I DO NOT HAVE TO BE HAUNTED BY WHAT MAY BE EXPOSED ABOUT ME, BECAUSE EVERYTHING THAT COULD EVER BE EXPOSED HAS ALREADY BEEN COVERED BY THE BLOOD OF JESUS.

If you're haunted by the fear of being known, you will live your life in hiding. You will become a master of nonanswers to personal questions. You will carry with you a catalog of platitudinous biblical responses that communicate to others that you are more spiritual than you actually are. I am persuaded that many pastors fear being known for who they really are and where they really struggle. I have had many pastors tell me they are afraid of their sin being exposed. They say that they can't be just normal sinners like everyone else. If we have produced a culture where pastors have to deny sin and live in fearful hiding, we have built a pastoral culture that cannot work, because it is a contradiction of the gospel that this culture is called to both proclaim and live.

I must remind myself that the gospel welcomes me out of hiding. It welcomes me to face my darkest parts with hope. It assures me that there is nothing to be known about me that has not already been dealt with in the person and work of the Lord Jesus. So I don't have to build my ministry on a lie that I am something I'm not. I can live in honesty and humility before others, entrusting my present and future ministry into the hands of my Savior, knowing that no matter how people respond to me, he will never turn his back on me or on the gifts that he has given me.

4) I NEED TO REMEMBER THAT MY WEAKNESSES ARE NOT IN THE WAY OF PRODUCTIVE MINISTRY, BUT MY DELUSIONS OF INDEPENDENT STRENGTH ARE.

You could argue that if human weakness was an automatic disqualifier from ministry, none of the disciples would have been called into ministry. The fact of the matter is that there is never a day, pastor, when you don't demonstrate somehow, someway that you are weak. There is never a day when you don't reveal that there are still pockets of foolishness in you. In fact, God will use the responsibilities, opportunities, burdens, and temptations of ministry to reveal to you and those who love you how weak you really are. He reveals your weakness to you so that you will continue to seek the help of his grace, and he reveals it to others so that they can be instruments of his grace in your life. Paul didn't resign his ministry because he became convinced he was the foremost of all sinners. No, you could argue that it is your admission of weakness that protects your ministry from becoming all about human reputation and kingdom building. And it is your weakness that protects you from the dangers of self-righteousness and self-reliance.

It is your delusions of perceived strength and maturity, which you actually lack, that have the potential to derail and ultimately destroy your ministry. This is because when you think you are strong, you think you can live independently of the grace of Jesus and the ministry of others, although you may not know that this is what you're doing.

5) I CAN REST ASSURED THAT GOD DIDN'T GET A WRONG ADDRESS WHEN HE CALLED ME TO MINISTRY. MY SPIRITUAL NEEDINESS DOESN'T COMPROMISE THE MESSAGE OF THE GOSPEL; RATHER, MY NEED PREACHES IT.

Now, let me say that it is obvious that you have to be at a certain level of maturity to qualify for ministry in the local church. What I think we need to address is the view that any weaknesses that are exposed in a pastor compromise or potentially make a mockery of the message he proclaims. If you take this view, you think that you have to present yourself as the perfect portrait of all that the gospel is able to produce or else you will bring shame to the name of Jesus. This leaves no room to admit and seek the help that you will invariably need as a pastor, since you are still right smack-dab in the middle of your own sanctification.

But, pastor, you will never be that perfect portrait; the only one who achieved that perfection was Christ. No, rather than being a perfect portrait that assures people that the gospel is true, you and I are called to be windows through which people look and see the glory of the risen Lord Jesus Christ. It is our weakness that demonstrates both the essentiality and power of the grace of the Lord Jesus Christ. Only his ever-present and powerful grace could enable a person, who still needs to be transformed himself, to be used as an instrument of his transforming grace in the lives of others. This frees us from pretending that we are what we are not. It frees us from boasting about what we could never have produced on our own, and it frees the people we serve from putting us on a messianic pedestal that should be reserved for Jesus only. We must preach to ourselves a gospel of ongoing weakness and sufficient grace.

6) THERE IS ONLY ONE MESSIAH, AND I AM DEFINITELY NOT HIM!

There is one thing that pastoral ministry makes very clear about us: we do not have the wisdom, character, and strength of the Messiah. It is okay to admit that we are not perfect in wisdom, that sometimes we are a fool. It is okay to admit that we are not complete in character, that there are moments when we lack the character that is needed. It is okay to admit that we fall short when it comes to strength; ministry will expose our weak places. If ministry has power to do anything in us, it has the power to destroy our naive trust in ourselves and to convince us that there is no solid rock of hope to be found but the rock Christ Jesus.

▲ ▲ ▲

You see, it is only the hope and surety of the gospel that can rescue you from both the duplicity and the idolatry that tempt every pastor. It is the courage of grace that will cause you to be willing to look at and deal with the places in your life where your message and your living are in disharmony. Only the gospel can free you from your futile attempts to make this separation work. And it is the irrevocable welcome of the gospel that frees you from seeking your identity and rest in things in your ministry that become your objects of functional worship but have no ability whatsoever to deliver what you're seeking. It is only the surety of God's boundless love that will free you from looking for comfort and hope in the false messiahs that greet every pastor.

There is a way in which pastoral ministry will make you either sad or delusional. Because ministry will expose your weakness, it has the power to produce in you a wholesome sadness, an abandonment of your own righteousness that will drive you to the cross for forgiveness, healing, and comfort. In gospel amnesia you will work to hide and deny what is being revealed and use the success of your public ministry persona to argue against what is being revealed in your private life. You will pursue and polish the delusion that you are a grace graduate when you are actually a case study of the need for the very things of the gospel that you offer to others. There may be only two roads for your heart to travel in ministry: the road of personal grief or the road of personal grandiosity. The first leads to greater hope in Christ and greater courage in ministry. The other leads to the pride of arrival, unwise choices, and trying to find independently a life that is only ever the result of living in gospel community with others. Grief will cause you to abandon your ministry-kingdom dreams for the purposes of a better King. Grandiosity will cause you to confuse your kingdom purposes with the King you have been called to serve. Grief will cause you to find joy in being an ambassador of the King of grace. Grandiosity will cause you to approach your ministry like a monarch who doesn't need grace. Pastor, be honest right here, right now—which pathway best describes your ministry?

CLOSING THE SEPARATION GAP

So if there are places in all of our lives as pastors where a separation exists between what we teach others and how we live, what can we do to close the gap? Let me suggest five commitments that should be nailed into each one of our ministry lives.

1) REQUIRE YOURSELF TO SIT UNDER YOUR OWN TEACHING AND PREACHING.

Our study for any moment of teaching or preaching must include personal application. We must ask ourselves what the particular passage we've been studying reveals about our own hearts. Where does this portion of God's Word call us to confession and repentance? What does it reveal about God's character and plan that should reignite our way of living? How should we apply its perspectives, principles, and commands to our daily lives? As we prepare, we need to give our hearts time to grieve our condition and celebrate the gospel. We need to take the time to pray words of confession and commit to concrete steps of repentance. We all need to take advantage of the huge blessing it is to be called by God to spend so much time in his freeing and transforming Word.

2) CONFESS PUBLICLY TO YOUR OWN STRUGGLE.

Now, I am not suggesting that you should air all of the stained linen of your heart every time you teach or preach. But I do think it is not only valuable for you but also important for your listeners to hear that you too have not arrived, that the life of faith is yet a struggle for you also. The very fact that you are baring your heart publicly closes the gap between your public persona and your private life. You are refusing to build a two-person existence. You are fighting against becoming comfortable with a disharmony between what you teach and how you live. You are applying your preaching and teaching before the eyes and ears of your congregation. You are inviting them in to pray for, confront, and encourage you, and you are publicly confessing that you are committed to living everything that you teach. You are publicly working to close the gap.

3) PLACE YOURSELF UNDER WISE AND BIBLICAL COUNSEL.

Pastor, it is plain and simple: you and I need to be pastored. One of the scandals of hordes of churches is that no one is pastoring their pastor. No one is helping him see what he is not seeing. No one is helping him examine his thoughts, desires, words, and behaviors. No one is regularly calling him to confession. No one is delineating where repentance is appropriate. No one is reaching into his discouragement with the truths of the presence, promises, and provisions of the Savior. No one is confronting his idolatry and pride. No one is alerting him to places of temptation and danger in his life.

Now, you and I don't have the liberty to just wait and hope that this happens. We need to take the initiative to seek out someone whom we respect and with whom we can build this kind of counseling relationship and commit to for the duration of our ministries. I am positing that it is not enough to do this in moments of personal discouragement and trouble. You and I need to humbly acknowledge that we need this kind of knowledgeable ministry relationship as a regular component of our ministries. In every ministry location I've been in, I have sought someone to pastor me. I can't imagine living my life or doing ministry without the protection, rescue, vision, and growth that this has provided for me. And I will confess that I need to be pastored today as much as I did years ago when I began to realize that, as a pastor, I had not been called or hardwired to go it on my own.

4) BE APPROACHABLE TO YOUR FRIENDS AND FAMILY.

There is another commitment that we need to make that has the power to close the separation gap that exists in the lives of way too many people in ministry: request the ministry of your family. Invite your spouse to point out areas of spiritual laziness and inconsistency. Invite your spouse to lovingly confront you when you are activating your inner lawyer and are unwilling to listen. Ask the one living closest to you about when you take out on your family the frustrations you have collected in your ministry. Ask for help in making better choices when it comes to being faithful to the dual calling you have to family and ministry. Invite your children to respectfully appeal to you when you have treated them in ways you would never treat someone in your church. No, we should not be parented by our children, but you and I should be humble and approachable, ready to admit that the way we exercise parental authority is not always a beautiful picture of the authority of God. Regularly ask your spouse or your children to pray for you. In times of family worship, ask for prayer where you are struggling. Commit to confessing your wrongs to the members of your family and seek their forgiveness. The question is this: are we open to the fact that no one has a better window on who we really are than the people we live with? Do we see this as a benefit and a blessing and therefore take personal, spiritual advantage of these relationships? Or are we failing to benefit from the insight of those living closest to us?

5) BUILD A HUMBLY CANDID LEADERSHIP COMMUNITY.

The fact is that many pastors are not known by their leaders, and many pastors don't really know their leaders. The fact is that in most leadership communities there is simply no time invested in forging a knowledgeable, mutually ministering leadership community. I am persuaded that your goal should be that your eldership, deaconate, or whatever other leadership group you have will be the most spiritually rich and helpful small group in your church. It should be that the other small groups would look at the spiritual community that you have forged with your leaders and say, "If only our small group could be like that!" Every time you gather, there should be appropriate confession and prayer. You should have leadership retreats for building those relationships with personal sharing, confession, and prayer. You should take advantage of ministry gatherings to seek prayer for areas where you are struggling or need growth. Remember, the ministries that you direct with your local leadership will never be shaped by the knowledge, skill, experience, and strategic planning of this leadership group. These ministries will be powerfully influenced by the condition of each of the hearts of those who lead. You and I must not let the business of the church destroy any hope that the leaders of the church will function as a vibrant spiritual community.

▲ ▲ ▲

Yes, there are still places in all of our lives where we are poor examples of what we hold out for others. There are places where we are not living up to the standard of what we teach and preach. This will be true until the Lord returns or takes us home, because God has chosen that our growth be a process, not an event. But here is the issue: have we learned how to be comfortable with the disconnect between ministry and life? Does this functional disharmony no longer bother us? Have we learned how to make our spiritual schizophrenia work? Or are we daily grieved by our inconsistency, and has our grief caused us to live and minister with greater humility and candor? Have we opened our lives to the help that God so graciously provides for all of us in his church? Here's the bottom line: do we live as though we really do think of ourselves, who have been called to pastor others, as people in need of pastoring ? Do we?

CHAPTER FIFTEEN

SO, WHAT NOW?

I will confess that this has been a very hard but very helpful book to write. God has used it to highlight many things in my heart—words and behavior that need attention. He has used it to expose attitudes and actions that are inconsistent with what I so passionately teach others. There have been many times during the writing that I have tried to share with Luella what God is showing me and have broken down in the process. There have been many times when I have had to push myself away from my writing and spend time in prayerful confession or in joyful personal celebration. I have been brought to see myself with greater accuracy and to a deeper gratitude for the unrelenting grace of my Savior. I have been humbled to see again why my standing with my Heavenly Father will never be based on my performance but on Christ's. And I have become less and less afraid of confessing to others that I am a man who is still in need of the Savior's rescue that comes to me through the ministry of his people.

So I want to leave you with a passage that is a wonderful summary of all that we have considered. It's Peter's counsel to church leaders found in 1 Peter 5:6–11:

> Humble yourselves, therefore, under the mighty hand of God so that at the proper time he may exalt you, casting all your anxieties on him, because he cares for you. Be sober-minded; be watchful. Your adversary the devil prowls around like a roaring lion, seeking someone to devour. Resist him, firm in your faith, knowing that the same kinds of suffering are being experienced by your brotherhood throughout the world. And after you have suffered a little while, the God of all grace, who has called you to his eternal glory in

> Christ, will himself restore, confirm, strengthen, and establish you. To him be the dominion forever and ever.

Let me delineate five directives from this passage that are a practical way of living out the call of this book.

1) KNOW YOUR PLACE.

It is a grief to me, but I must confess that as I look back on my years of ministry, I haven't always known my place. There have been moments, even seasons, when I have viewed my ministry as *my* ministry. It is now clear to me that some of the most significant periods of ministry hardship were God-sent to pry the grip of my hands off my ministry. A letter sent to fellow pastors questioning my orthodoxy, a vote that removed me from the Christian school that I had founded, and an influential local-church leader demeaning my preaching were all much more than the expected struggles of gospel ministry in a fallen world. No, I now know that they were the tools God employed to rescue my ministry and recapture my heart. They were the result not of God turning his back on me but of God turning his face of grace toward me. Perhaps the church had morphed into my little ministry kingdom. Perhaps the school had become *my* school. Perhaps I carried into the pulpit way too much pride in my preaching. God was not willing to squeeze his church into the tiny confines of my kingdom purposes. He was not willing to forsake his throne so that I could be the royal sovereign of my own ministry. He would not allow me to stand in the pulpit and be a glory thief. So he again and again has used hard ministry moments to reclaim my allegiance to his kingdom and glory.

This is the bottom line. This is the great internal war of ministry. You are called to be a public and influential ambassador of a glorious King, but you must resist the desire to be a king. You are called to trumpet God's glory, but you must never take that glory for yourself. You are called to a position of leadership, influence, and prominence, but in that position you are called to "humble yourself under the mighty hand of God" (v. 6). Perhaps there is nothing more important in ministry than knowing your place. Perhaps all the fear of man, the pride of knowing, the seduction of acclaim, the quest for control, the depression in the face of hardship, the envy of the ministry of others, the bitterness against detractors, and the anxiety of failure are all about the same thing. Each of these struggles is about the temptation to make your ministry about you. From that first dark moment in the garden, this has been the struggle—to make it all about us.

It is so easy to confuse your kingdom with the Lord's. It is so easy to tell yourself that you are fighting for the gospel when what you're really fighting for is your place. It is so easy to tell yourself that you're simply trying to be a good leader when what you really want is control. It is so easy to tell yourself that you want to build healthy ministry relationships when what you really want is for people to like you. It is so easy to tell yourself that you're trying to help people understand the details of their theology when what you're actually working to do is impress them with how much you know. It is so easy to tell yourself that you're fighting for what is right when what is really going on is that you're threatened by someone's rising influence. It's so easy to tell yourself that you just want what is best when what you really want is a comfortable and predictable ministry life. It is so easy to tell yourself that you want God to get glory when really you enjoy ministry celebrity more than you are willing to admit. It is hard to be in a position of ministry prominence and influence and to know your place. It is very tempting in subtle ways to want God's place. It is vital to realize that the temptation of the garden still lives in the pulpit, the study, the counseling office, and the ministry boardroom.

Here is the bottom line: wherever you are in ministry, whatever your position is, no matter how many people look up to you, whatever influence your ministry has collected, and no matter how long and successful your ministry has been, your ministry will never be about you because it is about him. God will not abandon his kingdom for yours. He will not offer up his throne to you. He will not give to you the glory that is his due. His kingdom and his glory are the hope of your ministry and the church. And when I forget my place and quest in some way for God's position, I place my ministry and the church that I have been called to serve in danger.

It is here that I need to be rescued from me. I can change ministry positions and locations, but I cannot escape the thoughts and desires of my own heart. So again this morning I cry out for the rescue of my Redeemer. I pray that he would fight on my behalf, that his grace would cause me to love him more than I love myself. I pray that he would give me such a profound satisfaction in his glory that I would have no interest in seeking my own. And as I pray, I know that I will need to pray this prayer again tomorrow, because tomorrow I will once again be tempted to lose my place and to make my ministry be the one thing it should never be—all about me.

In your ministry, in the location where God has positioned you, is there evidence that you have forgotten your place, or is your ministry shaped and protected by a daily commitment to "humble yourself under the mighty hand of God"? Would the people who serve with you think that you are too oriented toward power and control? Would the people you serve assess that you care too much about what people think about you? Would they say that you care too much about attention and influence? Would they characterize you as a humble servant leader? Would they see you as being tempted to take too much credit, or would they say that you clearly demonstrate that you know the ministry God has called you to is not about you? Would they conclude that you really do know your place?

2) REST IN GOD'S CARE.

Rest in God's care is the result of a functional, ministry-shaping belief that he really does care. There are moments in ministry when you will be tempted to wonder if God is near and if he cares. There will be moments when it will seem as if your prayers have gone unanswered. There will be moments of trial when it will seem as if God is absent. There will be moments when you will feel misunderstood and alone. There will be moments when it will be nearly impossible to figure out what in the world God is doing. There will be moments when you will be tempted to wonder if it's worth it, when selling iPads doesn't seem like such a bad idea. There will be moments when the bi-factorial pressure of ministry and family will seem too much to bear. There will be moments when it will feel as though God has given you neither the wisdom nor the strength to do what he's called you to do. There will be moments when opposition is great and progress is scarce. There will be moments when the temptation to doubt God's ever-present care will be great.

I have written about this before, but it is important to say it again. Even those of us in ministry get to the place where we are tempted to bring God into the court of our judgment and question his goodness, faithfulness, and love. There are times when you just want to scream, "Where are you?" or, "What in the world are you doing?" There are times when we are tempted to think that we would be a better head of the church than the one who is the Head, or a better sovereign than the Sovereign, or a better savior than the Savior. It is hard to admit, but there may be times when you wonder if God is asleep at the wheel.

The fact of the matter is that we will never figure God out. He will never do all the things that we were expecting. He will never stay on our agenda page. He will never be comfortably predictable. If we rest in God's care only when we understand just what he's doing, there will be many times and places where we won't rest in his care. The danger in all of this is this: we simply do not run for help to someone whom we have come to distrust. It is in the moments of hardship when what God is doing doesn't make any sense that it is all the more important to preach to ourselves the gospel of his unshakable, unrelenting, ever-present care. He *is* actively caring for you and me even in those moments when we don't understand his care and can't figure out what he is doing.

I will not tell myself that I am alone. I will not allow myself to think that I am poor. I will not give way to ministry panic or paralysis. I will not look for help where help cannot be found. God is with me, and he cares, and that guarantees that I do have and will have everything I need to be what I am called to be and to do what I have been chosen to do in the particular place of ministry to which he has appointed me.

Does your rest in God's care quiet your ministry anxiety? Does it keep you from feeling alone and overwhelmed? Does it comfort you in times of difficulty? Does your rest give rest and comfort to others? Does your rest in God's care keep you from feeling the need to escape in some way (food, chemicals, alcohol, sex, TV, Internet, activities, people, etc.)? Does your rest in God's care result in courage in ministry? Does it help you to deal humbly with opposition? At street level, do you rest in God's care?

3) TAKE YOUR MINISTRY SERIOUSLY.

It's almost as if Peter is saying, "Have you forgotten the existence of real, personal evil? Have you forgotten that ministry is a constant, moment-by-moment spiritual war? Have you become comfortable with not taking this spiritual war seriously in the context of your daily life and ministry? Have you forgotten that this side of eternity you and your people are under incessant spiritual attack? Is your attitude toward your ministry all too casual? Do you allow yourself to do things you would not do if you thought that you were involved in the most important war that has ever been fought? Are there essential things that you fail to do because you have not taken the spiritual war of ministry seriously?"

It's sad and dangerous, but it's true that many of us have taken on a functionally unspiritual view of our ministries. We have a street-level view of the ministry of the local church that is more about staffing, strategic plans, building programs, financial planning, corporate structures, audience demographics, cultural relevance, career advancement, budget maintenance, resourcing initiatives, etc., than about how best to be good soldiers in the great spiritual war that is waged inside and outside of us. Perhaps it is this deeply unspiritual view of ministry that sets up many of us for trouble, because it exposes too many of us to temptation. You would think that the last thing Peter would have to tell leaders in Christ's church is that they need to be watchful because there really is a Devil, but he does.

Peter knew the trap that many of us have fallen into, that in the midst of ministry we forget who we are, forget the condition of the world we live in, and forget who the people we have been called to serve are, and in forgetting we lose sight of evil on the attack that is the context in which all of us minister. Pastor, your theology won't prevent you from being spiritually attacked. Your gifts don't put you in a position of being free from attack. Your experience won't defend you against attack. Proper staffing and good strategic plans won't alleviate the spiritual realities that Peter here warns us to attend to. There is a devouring Devil. You need to be serious and watchful.

There have been very few pastors whose ministries have been damaged by poor strategic planning. There are very few pastors whose ministries have been compromised by poor staffing. There are very few pastors who have lost their way in ministry because they didn't budget well. But there are thousands of pastors who have damaged or destroyed their ministries because they lost sight of what ministry was really about and did not protect themselves against temptation and, sadly, became casualties of the very war that Peter says we should never forget.

If you really do believe what Peter says about everyday ministry in the local church, then there are things you will constantly do. You will look out for the seductive and tempting lies of the enemy. You will never think that you've risen to a point where you no longer have to be careful. You will make sure that as a pastor, you are being pastored. You will surround yourself with people to whom you can freely confess your weaknesses, failures, struggles, and sins. You will invite people to confront, warn, challenge, and rebuke you when necessary, and you will not be defensive and self-righteous when they do. You will commit to a daily nurture of your own soul. You will look for evidences of the Devil's hand in your staff and your leaders. You will set limits for yourself—boundaries that others help you maintain to protect you from you. You will be watchful for inconsistencies between your public ministry persona and your private life. You will go back again and again to 1 Peter 5 with your staff and leaders. You will require that the way you approach ministry, even in the most mundane places, be formed by Peter's words of warning.

4) RESIST, NO MATTER WHAT.

Peter says something here that seems strange at first glance. He exhorts us in ministry to resist the Devil, and then he says, ". . . knowing that the same kinds of suffering are being experienced by your brotherhood throughout the world" (v. 9). These words reveal that Peter is a wise and insightful pastor himself. After calling those of us in ministry to resist the Devil, that is, to not give way to anything that would give him room to do his devouring work, he then exposes one of the Devil's most seductive lies. The Devil wants you to think that your ministry is particularly difficult. He wants you to think that you have been singled out for unique suffering. He wants you to begin to believe that your ministry situation, location, and relationships are definitely more difficult than what others face. He wants you to buy into the lie that while you're suffering, they're thriving; while you're being questioned, they're being respected; and while your work is hard, their work is easy. He wants to get you to begin to carry around the burden that somehow, someway, you've been singled out.

And why does the Devil want to get you to think that you have been chosen for particular suffering? He does because he wants you to do the one thing that will weaken you and ultimately destroy your ministry. He wants you to begin to question the presence, goodness, faithfulness, and grace of God. This is his most powerful weapon. It has the power to hurt you and your ministry. You see, if you have come to doubt the goodness of God, in your moment of need you won't run to him, because you tend not to run for help to someone you have come to doubt. And if you have come to question the goodness of God, it makes it very hard to call others to entrust themselves to his goodness. Harboring fundamental personal questions about the goodness of God will suck the spiritual vitality out of you and your ministry. And it should be noted that you can still be involved in day-by-day ministry and still be holding onto your formal theological confession and yet be a person who, in the recesses of your heart, has come to question the faithfulness of God. There are many angry and bitter pastors who are cranking it out with no thought of resigning but wonder if the God they've been called to represent really does care.

There is something else that needs to be observed here. Peter is not surprised that his readers are suffering, and he's not surprised that their brothers in ministry are suffering, because he knows from firsthand experience that being called to ministry is at once being called to suffer (see 2 Corinthians 1 for Paul's discussion of this). Just as every soldier in every war suffers in some way, so pastors in the great spiritual war of redemption will suffer in some way. Perhaps the military man doesn't suffer injury, but he will suffer the suspension of his life, he will suffer separation from his loved ones, he will suffer the fear, tension, and exhaustion of battle, he will suffer the horror of seeing and experiencing things that no human should, and he will be hit with the guilt of being a survivor who wishes he could have done more. In the same way, gospel ministry puts you on the front line and exposes you to the personal and corporate dangers of war. It is impossible to be in ministry and not be affected. So you and I must resist the lie of the enemy that we have been selected to face what others haven't. We must resist the temptation of thinking that God has forgotten us, neglected us, or turned his back on us. We must refuse to feel that we are victims of abandonment by the One we are called to represent. And we must remember that our suffering is not in the way of God's plan, but part of it. In our suffering God is not only with us but also is employing it to change us and those to whom we minister.

5) TRUST GOD'S SANCTIFYING GRACE.

Peter ends his call to church leaders by reminding them not of what they have been called to but of what they have been given. In so doing, he points them to the only place where they will ever find rest, hope, security, inner peace, and a reason to continue.

When in your ministry you begin to look horizontally for what you have already been given vertically, you place yourself and your ministry in spiritual danger. When you look to your ministry to give you identity instead of ministering out of the identity that you have already been given, you introduce a neediness and anxiety that will weaken and misdirect your ministry. When people's respect and esteem are what keep you going rather than God's unrelenting, ever-present grace, you will end up being disappointed and discouraged and wondering if you've got what it takes to continue. When you look to your own resources of wisdom and strength, needing to be more righteous than you actually are, you set yourself up for failure because you do not reach out for moment-by-moment grace.

So Peter ends his words of wisdom, warning, and comfort with the bottom line for everyone in ministry. You have one—and only one—place to look for your rest, motivation, and hope. You cannot search for these things in yourself, in the people you serve, in the leaders who serve with you, or in your ministry success. You and I must preach an ancient gospel of grace to ourselves with fresh application and enthusiasm day after ministry day. We must not evaluate ourselves solely on the basis of our gifts and track record. We must not assess our future based on the response we are currently getting.

It is interesting that Peter feels the need to call ministers of the gospel to remember the gospel. You would think this wouldn't be necessary, but it is. Perhaps this is the only thing that this book you have just read is about. It is a detailed exposition of what happens in the life of a person in ministry when he forgets to preach to himself the same gospel that he gives to others. It is sad, but true, that there are thousands of gospel ministers whose lives and ministries are shaped by a functional gospel amnesia. Because it is, these leaders and the ministries they serve are paying the price that comes when you look for life where it cannot be found.

Peter is not at all hesitant or embarrassed to preach the gospel one more time to ministers of the gospel. He knows that in the ardor, struggle, and suffering of local-church ministry, often the gospel is one of the first casualties. So he starts by reminding his readers that grace guarantees their future. He says, "You have been called to eternal glory in Christ" (see v. 10). Now, it is important to understand why this is not just a distant hope but a motivation for ministry right here, right now. Here's Peter's logic. If you and I have been guaranteed a place in eternity with our Savior, then we also have been guaranteed all the grace we need along the way. The promise of future grace always carries with it the promise of present grace. If the end of my story is secure, it means God cannot abandon or lose me along the way. Pastor, your eternal future carries with it the sure promise that you will have all the grace you need to do what you've been called to do between the time you came to Christ and the time you will go home to be with him forever.

But Peter says even more. He wants you to know that your Lord isn't only protecting, providing for, and enabling you, but he is working to change you as well. There is never a moment in ministry when you aren't being ministered to. The Savior is not just working through you in the lives of others, but he is also working in you as he works through you. He is not just calling you to be an agent of his transforming grace; he is transforming you by the same grace. He is not just committed to the success of your ministry but also to the triumph of his grace in your own heart and life. So, he says, "Christ . . . will himself restore, confirm, strengthen, and establish you" (v. 10). You are never just a vehicle of his amazing grace. No, you are always also a recipient of that grace. In your heart of hearts you know you desperately need everything you tell others that God has committed himself in Christ to give them. Well, Peter wants you to be assured once again that you are still the objects of his redeeming care and that you will continue to be until that care has completed its work. Now, that gives you reason to get up in the morning and continue even when your sin and weaknesses have been exposed and ministry is hard.

But Peter has one final punch line. He is eager to remind you that your Savior has dominion forever and ever. The One you look to for hope has absolute rulership over every ministry situation in which you'll find yourself. It is impossible to ever be in a ministry situation, location, or relationship that is not ruled by King Christ. Here's why this is so important: all of his promises to you depend on his sovereignty. He is only able to guarantee the delivery of his promises in the places where he has complete control. And since he has complete control over everything, there is no place in ministry where you will be unable to depend on the delivery of everything he has promised you. Also, the hope for your ministry is not the success of your pastoral control or ingenuity but that a sovereign Savior will complete his plan for his church. So where do we go from here?

In your place of ministry, commit to regularly preach Peter's gospel to yourself and ask those around you to remind you of it again and again. If you are a seminary, denominational, or ministry leader, work with others to address the places where your ministry training and culture are less than biblical. If you're in ministry and these pages have exposed your heart, confess what needs to be confessed and seek help. If you're a pastor and you have come to see how your ministry culture needs change, address those issues with your leaders and make those changes with them.

If you've read this book because you love your pastor or ministry leader and are concerned for him, pray daily for him and seek to encourage him in the gospel wherever and whenever it is appropriate to do so. If you're the spouse of someone in ministry and are concerned for his spiritual welfare, don't sit by in silence, don't lash out in discouragement and anger, but confront and encourage him to seek help. And as you do these things, remember these words: "Now may the God of peace who brought again from the dead our Lord Jesus, the great shepherd of the sheep, by the blood of the eternal covenant, equip you with everything good that you may do his will, working in us that which is pleasing in his sight, through Jesus Christ, to whom be glory forever and ever. Amen" (Heb. 13:20–21).

GENERAL INDEX

SCRIPTURE INDEX